Bridge: Basic Defence

Bridge: Basic Defence

Freddie North

B. T. Batsford Ltd, *London*

First published 1997

ISBN 0 7134 8244 3

Typeset by Apsbridge Services Ltd, Nottingham.

Printed by Redwood Books, Trowbridge, Wiltshire
for the publishers,
B. T. Batsford Ltd, 583 Fulham Road,
London SW6 5BY

A BATSFORD BRIDGE BOOK
Series Editor: Tony Sowter

CONTENTS

INTRODUCTION

The game of bridge is divided into three separate parts, Bidding, Play and Defence, and since you will be defending at least twice as often as you will be playing it is clearly vital that you are fully conversant with all the helpful guides that can be made available to you.

It is generally accepted that defence is harder than declarer play, but it can be just as much fun and the very fact that it is more demanding makes the rewards particularly succulent.

When the dummy goes down the declarer knows exactly the forces that are pitted against him, but this is not the case with a defender who sees just one of the opponent's hands (the dummy) and has to assess the disposition of the outstanding cards. Then there is the question of collaborating with partner. This is not a problem for the declarer but imposes quite a strain on many partnerships – even those with considerable experience.

By the time you have digested the hints and advice in this book I am sure you will be a much more competent defender. You will be well capable of visualising declarer's plan and then taking the necessary steps to sabotage it. Of course, you will also know how to help your partner. But what about partner? It can be a very frustrating experience defending with an untutored accomplice, so perhaps you could lend your own partner this book or in the last resort he or she might even go to the shops and ....

Good luck and have lots of fun, for that is what bridge is all about whether you are playing the hand or defending it.

Freddie North
July 1997

1
THE OPENING LEAD

The defenders enjoy one major advantage and that is the choice of opening lead. The responsibility for initiating the attack is given to the player on declarer's left and many a contract fails or succeeds as a result of the choice that is made.

To select consistently good opening leads it is necessary to listen carefully to the bidding. The opposition inevitably have to reveal some of their secrets and, indeed, partner will sometimes be a significant contributor. If there are no helpful clues forthcoming (e.g. 1NT-3NT) then the player on lead should at least know the standard approach.

The choice of card is usually dictated by a popular and largely recognised formula (a full table of standard leads appears at the end of this chapter), but the choice of suit – ah, that's a different matter. Nevertheless, certain card combinations are so clearly more attractive than others that most defenders will readily plump for the norm which is likely to be correct most of the time. For example, choosing between two suits like this, AKQ6 or AJ96, it is not difficult to see that the former offers a safer and more productive line of attack.

Leading against suit contracts, no trumps or slams all have different priorities and in the final analysis may call for some exceptional treatment. However, you may find these guidelines useful.

Leading against a Suit Contract

The main aim is not to give away unnecessary tricks, thus the best leads are usually from the top of a high three-card honour sequence (AKQ, KQJ, QJ10), or partner's suit. A singleton is particularly attractive when it is hoped to obtain a ruff, or ruffs, but this lead can do more harm than good if it is clear from the bidding, and your own hand, that partner cannot possibly obtain the lead.

Defending against 4♠ by South, West holds one of the following hands:

(a)	West	South	North
	♠ K64	1♠	3♠
	♡ AQ542	4♠	
	◊ 6		
	♣ KQ105		

East is marked with a near-Yarborough so it would be very optimistic to hope that he could obtain the lead and give you a diamond ruff. Lead the ♣K.

(b)	West	South	North
	♠ K64	1♠	3♠
	♡ Q8643	4♠	
	◊ 6		
	♣ 10653		

Now the singleton diamond has much more chance of succeeding and easily rates as the best lead.

Leading partner's suit cannot be emphasised strongly enough, especially when he has made an overcall. Indeed, he may have bid with this very point in mind. Even when leading partner's suit turns out to be an inferior defence you can approach the post mortem with justifiable confidence!

Against a suit contract, underleading an ace (playing a low card from, say A9642) as the initial gambit is generally a poor idea. It is seldom profitable and can be very costly. As the role of an ace is to capture a lower honour (usually a king or queen) it is best to look elsewhere for your opening attack, but if you must play this suit then lead the ace.

The lead of the ace from a suit headed by the AK (AK974) is usually sound. If you decide to lead from a broken suit then choose the fourth highest (KJ642), the four.

Defending against 4♡ by South, West holds:

West	South	North
♠ Q6	1♡	2◇
♡ J86	2♡	4♡
◇ Q83		
♣ KJ643		

No lead is particularly attractive but the ♣4 (fourth highest) appears to offer the best prospects. If West's clubs were headed by the AK then the ♣A would be more or less automatic.

Don't lead a singleton trump as it may damage your partner's holding. One exception is when the opponents have shown an especially strong trump suit (e.g. 2♠-4♠) and a lead from any other suit might concede an unnecessary trick.

Defending against 4♠ by South, West holds the following hands:

(a) West	South	North
♠ 4	2♠	4♠
♡ AJ943		
◇ K75		
♣ KJ63		

Lead ♠4. In this case the lead of the singleton spade is unlikely to do any harm because it is inconceivable that declarer has a trump loser. Anything else may cost.

(b) West	South	North
♠ 4	1♠	2◇
♡ AJ943	2♠	3♠
◇ Q92	4♠	
♣ Q1064		

Lead ♣4. This time there is a distinct possibility that a spade lead will kill a critical holding in partner's hand, say Qxx or J10xx.

A trump lead can be effective when it is necessary to cut down dummy's ruffing power. Play low from two or three small (93, 972) also from J105.

Defending against 4♡ by South, West, apparently, has an unattractive lead.

West		South	North
♠ AJ97		1♠	2◇
♡ 973		2♡	3♡
◇ 86		4♡	
♣ A1054			

However, if there is a singleton spade in dummy declarer will no doubt wish to ruff some of his spade losers. Sabotage his plan by leading the ♡3.

With a doubleton, except in the trump suit, lead the higher card (K6, J5, 97, 42) but play the middle card from three small, following next time with the highest card (963) to differentiate from a doubleton. This is called MUD, Middle, Up, Down.

Partner leads the 8 and follows next time with the 5. He probably has a doubleton.

Partner leads the 6 and follows next time with the 8. He probably has a trebleton.

You should lead the lowest from a three or four card suit headed by an honour (K64, Q1052, J72, 1063), but the highest when two touching honours are involved (KQ743, QJ963, J105).

It is worth noting that when partner leads a small card (assuming you can rule out a singleton) he is usually leading away from an honour holding.

If partner leads the 2 (K1062) he has probably led from a four-card suit headed by an honour.

If partner leads the 4 (Q9642) and the 3 is on view he has probably led from a 4 or 5 card suit headed by an honour (assuming you can rule out a singleton or 42 doubleton).

The correct lead from a suit with an interior honour sequence is the top of the sequence (KJ1096, Q1097) and, if you have to lead from four small, the second highest is traditional (8642). On the next round you follow with the highest card if you can afford it.

It is usually advantageous to lead a long suit when your own holding in trumps is substantial, say, K1086 or AJ93.

West	South	North
♠ KJ97	1♠	2♡
♡ 74	2♠	3♠
◊ KJ8643	4♠	
♣ 5		

Defending against 4♠ it would be a mistake to play for ruffs by leading your singleton club. Much better to plug away at your long suit and hope to weaken declarer's trump holding. Lead the ◊ 6.

Leading against a No Trump Contract

The priorities are now rather different as the main aim is to build up enough defensive tricks to defeat the contract before declarer can establish sufficient winners. Often this entails giving away a trick (or more) in order to set up your own, or partner's, suit. Of course, the top of a sequence (KQJ95) is normally more attractive than the fourth highest of a broken suit (K8643).

Although the lead of a small card from something like AJ852, or indeed AK852, would be viewed as suicidal against a suit contract, it would be perfectly normal against a no trump contract.

Defending against 3NT by South, West should lead the ♡6.

West	South	North
♠ 842	1NT	3NT
♡ AK863		
◊ J105		
♣ 74		

This gives West the best chance of setting up his suit while at the same time retaining a link with his partner's hand.

When you are considering your lead remember that partner's suit should still be given a high priority, especially if he has made an overcall.

West		West	North	East	South
♠ Q63		–	1◇	1♡	1♠
♡ 106		Pass	2◇	Pass	2NT
◇ 853		Pass	3NT	All Pass	
♣ KJ854					

Without partner's overcall you would have led the ♣5, but in view of his bid of 1♡ you should lead the ♡10.

If one of the opponents has bid your longest suit, and partner has not bid, it may be best to try and 'find' partner's suit. For example, holding:

♠ 1096
♡ K6
◇ Q8643
♣ 752

with diamonds having been bid on your right and hearts on your left, my choice of opening would be the ♠10. And if the spades were, say, 962 I would choose the ♠9 as it is inadvisable to play MUD against no trump contracts. Faced with a choice between a major and a minor suit lead, it is usually best to choose the major. The reason for this is that while, opponents will frequently suppress a minor suit in the bidding, they will be less likely to do so in the case of a major.

The top of the interior sequence is best in holdings like these:

AJ1096   KJ1084   Q10985   AQJ1086

Standard Opening Leads against Suit Contracts

Top of honour sequence
or near sequence
AKQxx
KQJx
QJ10
J109x
1098x
AKxxx
KQxx
KQ10x
QJ9x
J108x
AKx but K
fromAK alone

MUD from three small
(Middle, Up, Down):
963
874
752

Higher of two except
when trumps:
96
74
32
K8
A5
Q6
103

Low from two or three trumps:
94
73
862
K83
J105

Top of interior sequence
headed by an honour:
KJ109
Q1097

Lowest of three when
headed by an honour:
K73
Q104
J95
1062

Fourth highest from long
broken suit:
KJ742
Q743
J964
10863
Q106432

Standard Opening Leads Against No Trump Contracts

Top of sequence or
near sequence:

AKQxxx
KQJxx
QJ10xx
J109xxx
AKJxxx
KQ10xx
QJ9xx
J108xx

Fourth highest of longest
and strongest suit:

A10754
KJ8632
Q8632
107532
965432
AK653
QJ542
K987

Top of interior sequence
headed by an honour:

AQJ10xx
AJ109x
KJ108x
Q109xx

Higher or highest of two or
three small cards:

74
86
863
752

This lead is usually made
when the bidding suggests
that any alternative is even
more unattractive – or when
partner has bid the suit.

Lowest from three to an honour:

A83
K96
Q102
J74
1063

An unattractive lead unless the
bidding suggests otherwise.

Leads against Small Slams in a Suit

Although it is difficult to generalise, it is usually best to attack against a small slam in a suit unless partner is marked with a worthless hand. In each of the following cases it is assumed that the suit from which it is recommended that the lead be made has not been bid as a genuine suit by either opponent.

1.
West
♠ 3
♡ A64
◊ 9852
♣ Q10753

Against 6♠ or 6♡, lead the ♣5. This may be your best chance to set up a winner before the ♡A is knocked out.

2.
West
♠ 64
♡ Q73
◊ A862
♣ 8643

Against 6♠ lead the ♡3 for the same reason as in No. 1.

3.
West
♠ K6
♡ 986
◊ QJ75
♣ K1086

Against 6♠ lead the ♡9. You have too much to warrant an attacking lead. Partner must hold a near-Yarborough so play safe with a negative lead.

4.   **West**
                                  ♠ K642
                                  ♡ –
                                  ◇ 863
                                  ♣ 1076432

Against 6♡ lead the ♠2. It is best to attack and try to develop a spade trick. Maybe partner will make a trump trick.

Leads against Small Slams in No Trumps

Against small slams in no trumps it usually pays to make a safe lead, especially when the bidding has indicated two balanced hands.

1.	West		South	North
	♠ Q74		2NT	4NT
	♡ J963		6NT	
	◇ Q642			
	♣ 97			

It is too dangerous to lead from the honour holdings, so lead the ♣9.

2.	West		South	North
	♠ J743		1NT	6NT
	♡ K6			
	◇ 875			
	♣ Q1064			

Again you should make a safe lead. Either the ◇8 or ◇7 is likely to work out best.

3. | West | South | North |
    | --- | --- | --- |
    | ♠ Q106 | 2◇ | 2♡ |
    | ♡ 742 | 3◇ | 4◇ |
    | ◇ 85 | 4NT | 5◇ |
    | ♣ A8532 | 6NT | |

Lead the ♠6. This time declarer has not got a balanced hand, that is why you are advised to attack with a spade lead, as you would against 6◇.

Leads against Grand Slams

Against a grand slam in either a suit or in no trumps always make as safe a lead as possible. You don't need to establish a trick – you just need to avoid giving one away.

1.   **West**
                                    ♠ Q1074
                                    ♡ J5
                                    ◇ J109
                                    ♣ 7642

Against 7NT lead the ◇ J.

2.   **West**
                                    ♠ J753
                                    ♡ Q8
                                    ◇ 753
                                    ♣ J852

Against 7◇ lead a trump, often a good lead against a grand slam.

2
SECOND HAND
PLAYS LOW

The advice that the second hand should play low, while the third hand should play high, is a throwback to the days of whist. As a generalisation it is sound enough but it should not be regarded as a hard and fast rule for there are many exceptions, some quite obvious, some more obscure. The reason for playing low as second player is easily demonstrated by the following examples:

(a)

Dummy
962

Q10854   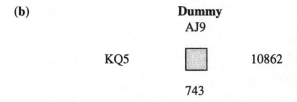   A73

KJ

The two is led from dummy towards the closed hand. If East hops up with the ace South has no guess and loses just one trick. If, however, East follows the general advice of 'second player plays low', South is immediately faced with a losing option. If he decides to insert the jack he will lose two tricks.

(b)

Dummy
AJ9

KQ5   10862

743

South leads the three towards dummy. If West plays low South will probably opt for the percentage shot of the nine, losing two tricks in the suit. Of course, if West requires just one quick trick in the suit he would no doubt split his honours.

(c)

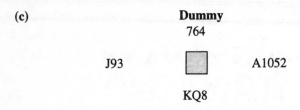

Dummy
764

J93   A1052

KQ8

The four is led from dummy towards the closed hand. If East goes up with the ace South's problems are over, but if he plays low on the first round South will have to utilise a further entry to dummy in order to make the two tricks to which he is entitled.

(d)

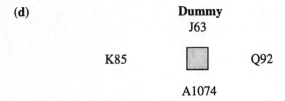

Dummy
J63

K85   Q92

A1074

South plays a low card towards dummy. If West gets itchy fingers and plays his king, declarer will be able to make three tricks in the suit via a simple finesse through East on the next round, but if West plays low the defence will come to two tricks in the suit.

Even when the cards are distributed as follows West does best to duck on the first round:

(e)

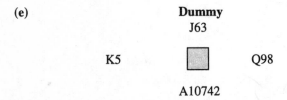

Dummy
J63

K5   Q98

A10742

South plays a low card towards dummy and if West's nerves are good enough he will duck at normal tempo. East will win this trick and subsequently West may score his king as declarer goes to dummy and finesses East for the king. If, however, West goes up with the king on the first round there will be no more losers in the suit when declarer finesses East for the queen.

Of course, commonsense must always prevail regardless of slogans, popular doctrine and folklore, so that if you were defending against 7NT and held an ace as second player it would be ludicrous to play low. That could easily be your last chance of defeating the contract. Exactly the same argument applies to lower-level contracts where the first duty of the defending side is to defeat the contract.

3
THIRD HAND PLAYS HIGH

The idea of contributing a high card as third player is based on the concept that it may subsequently promote winners for your side – usually for your partner. Declarer has to spend one of his high cards to win the trick and that may leave your side's intermediates playing a powerful role.

Study the following examples:

(a)

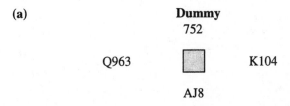

Dummy
752

Q963   K104

AJ8

West leads the three and East, as third player, must follow with the king. South takes his ace but now his J8 will be trapped under West's Q9. Should East make the mistake of playing a pusillanimous ten on the first round South will make an additional trick.

(b)

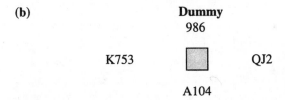

Dummy
986

K753   QJ2

A104

Against a no trump contract by South, West leads the three of this suit. Of course East must play a high card, but which one? If he were leading he would play the queen, but in third position he should play the lowest, or lower of equals, the jack in this case (the 10 with QJ10). When the jack forces declarer's ace, West will know that his partner holds the queen, but not the ten. If East mistakenly plays the queen on the first round West will place South with the jack and will be completely in the dark about the ten.

(c)   **Dummy**
                                                87

A10643   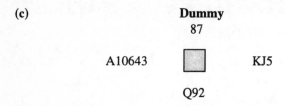   KJ5

                                                Q92

Against a no trump contract West makes the standard lead of the four and you can see from the above diagram that it is essential for East to play the king. If he fails to do so declarer will score his queen to which he is not entitled. There is no point in East playing the jack because even if South does have the AQ the king is dead anyway.

(d)   **Dummy**
                                                852

K103   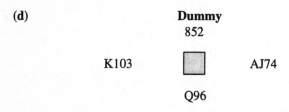   AJ74

                                                Q96

West leads the three and East must play the ace (third player plays high), otherwise South will make his queen.

4
THIRD HAND PLAYS INTERMEDIATE

Despite everything that has been said about the third hand playing high there are many occasions when an intermediate card is correct. This card is usually the second highest. The clue that should guide a defender is what appears in dummy. If there are only small cards on the table, then the third player invariably plays high, but if there is an honour card, or cards, then the third player usually gains by playing an intermediate card.

In the following examples East can assume that his partner's lead is from a holding headed by an honour. The bidding, which is always the key in these situations, precludes the possibility of it being a singleton:

(a) West leads the two, dummy plays the four and East ...?

Dummy
Q84

K972   ☐   AJ6

1053

East must play the knave. The defence will now score three tricks in the suit. If East makes the mistake of contributing any other card it will cost a trick. Say he plays the ace, now dummy's queen will eventually become a trick for declarer.

(b) West leads the three, dummy plays the nine and East ...?

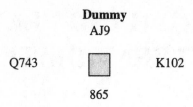

> **Dummy**
> AJ9
>
> Q743   K102
>
> 865

East should play the ten. West's lead (a small card from an honour holding) almost certainly marks him with the queen. If East makes the mistake of playing the king on the nine the defence will score just that one trick instead of the two to which they are entitled.

(c) West leads the four, dummy plays the two and East ...?

> **Dummy**
> Q72
>
> J654   K109
>
> A83

West will not have led from an ace against a suit contract so his honour will be the jack, thus East must play the nine (the lower of equals – the ten would deny the nine). When West gets in again and continues this suit the defence will come to two tricks.

(d) West leads the two, dummy plays the four and East ...?

> **Dummy**
> Q64
>
> 10752   KJ8
>
> A93

East should play the jack which will force the ace and leave the king as master. There is no certainty that the defence will now come to two tricks but if declarer has to continue this suit himself that is exactly what will happen.

(e) West leads the ten, dummy plays the three and East ...?

Dummy
J53

K1097   Q82

A64

East must play a low card. Only if dummy contributes the jack should East play the queen.

(f) West leads the two, dummy plays the nine and East ...?

Dummy
AQ9

J742   K105

863

East should play the ten. It is more than likely that West holds the jack.

(g) West leads the four, dummy plays the nine and East ...?

Dummy
Q95

K864   AJ10

732

East must play the ten. If West has led from the king, the defence will take all the tricks in this suit. If South happens to have the king, he will win this trick, but when West leads the suit again East will score two tricks.

(h) West leads the two, dummy plays the three and East ...?

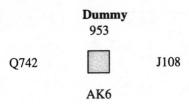

Dummy
953

Q742   J108

AK6

East should play the eight because the nine is in the dummy. When South wins with the ace or king West will know that East holds the J10 and will be able to continue the suit safely.

(i) Against a no trump contract West leads the four, dummy plays the three and East ...?

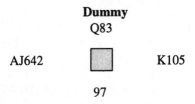

Dummy
Q83

AJ642   K105

97

East should play the ten. If South has the jack one trick will have to be lost anyway, but if West's suit is headed by the AJ the defence will take all the tricks.

(j) Against a no trump contract West leads the four, dummy plays the five and East ...?

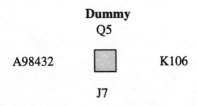

Dummy
Q5

A98432   K106

J7

This time East should play the king in case the cards lie as illustrated. If South had Ax, or Axx, he would have put up dummy's queen.

5

COVERING AN HONOUR
WITH AN HONOUR
AND WHEN NOT TO

Unfortunately there is no hard and fast rule that tells you precisely when you should cover an opponent's honour card, and when you shouldn't. However, it is well worth noting the following simple guide lines which will stand you in good stead most of the time.

Always cover an honour with an honour if there is any prospect of your side gaining a trick as a result. Never cover if the bidding, or obvious distribution of the cards, suggests that there is nothing to be won by covering.

The following examples will help to clarify. In each case the suit illustrated is a side suit, not the trump suit which is dealt with separately. If you want to play it the hard way cover up the West and South hands.

(a) The jack is led from dummy. Should East cover or play low?

Dummy
J7

9542   ◻   K83

AQ106

When trying to decide whether to cover or not, a defender must forget about 'Second Player Plays Low' and instead rely on the general guide lines concerning the covering of honours. Here, East should cover the jack with the king (cover if your side might gain a trick) because, although he can't promote a trick for himself, he may be able to do so for his partner. If East fails to cover, declarer will repeat the finesse and then, when the king drops under the ace on the third round, declarer will have four winners. Note the difference if the jack is covered by the king. The AQ10 all win but now West's nine will beat South's six.

(b) The queen is led from dummy. Should East cover or play low?

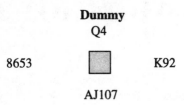

Dummy
Q4

8653   K92

AJ107

This is a similar position to (a). If East covers with the king he will save a trick.

(c) The jack is led from dummy. Should East cover?

Dummy
J1097

8   Q642

AK53

It would be quite wrong for East to cover as there is no way to promote or develop a defensive trick by so doing.

(d) The queen is led from dummy. Should East cover?

Dummy
QJ2

1075   K63

A984

East should not cover the first honour (Q) but must cover the second honour (J) when it is played next. Suppose the play to the first trick goes Q,K,A,5. Now declarer can lead the nine and finesse West's ten. This way declarer makes all four tricks in the suit. But when the queen is allowed to win and the jack is then covered by the king, West's ten becomes master. The general rule in these situations is to cover the second honour, not the first, although there are a few exceptions.

(e) The jack is led from dummy. Should East cover?

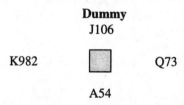

Dummy
J106

K982   Q73

A54

The general rule of covering the second honour, not the first, pays a dividend here. If East makes the mistake of covering the jack, declarer will make two tricks, but if East waits for the second honour declarer will be held to just one trick.

When a defender has two honours, or when he has a doubleton headed by an honour it may be necessary to cover the first honour played.

(f) The ten is led from dummy. Which card should East play?

Dummy
1093

A874   KJ5

Q62

East should play the jack, denying declarer a single trick in the suit.

(g) The jack is led from dummy. Should East cover?

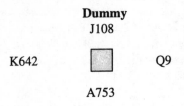

Dummy
J108

K642   Q9

A753

East should cover the jack with the queen. This may result in the defence making two tricks. If the first trick goes J,9,3,K that is the only trick the defence will make in this suit. If the play goes J,Q,A,2, declarer may finesse the 8 on the next round.

(h) Declarer leads the queen. Should West cover?

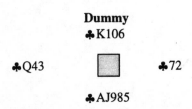

Dummy
AJ1086

K7532   9

Q4

West should play low. There is nothing to be gained by covering.

(i) Clubs have been bid by South who subsequently finishes in 3NT. Having won the first trick in hand, declarer plays the ♣J. Should West cover?

Dummy
♣K106

♣Q43   ♣72

♣AJ985

South is fishing, hoping for a cover! Don't play his game as nothing can be gained by playing your queen. But remember to play a low card smoothly. If you hesitate first and then play low you might as well show declarer your cards.

(j) South leads the queen. Should West cover?

Dummy
A52

K743 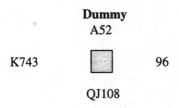 96

QJ108

West should play low as his king cannot be caught. The same would apply
if dummy had Ax and West had Kxx.

(k) West leads the ♡Q which holds the trick. Hearts are continued to
dummy's ace and declarer then plays the ◇Q. Should East cover?

Dummy
♠ AK1086
♡ A3
◇ QJ4
♣ K86

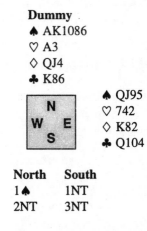

♠ QJ95
♡ 742
◇ K82
♣ Q104

North	South
1♠	1NT
2NT	3NT

Despite the general advice to cover the second honour the priorities in this
case are a little different. West is trying to establish his heart suit and
anything East can do to help will be in their mutual interests. If West has
the ◇A it is imperative that East wins the first round so that he can clear
the heart suit while West retains his card of entry. If it turns out that South
has the ◇A then nothing will be lost by East covering on the first round.

The full deal might be like this:

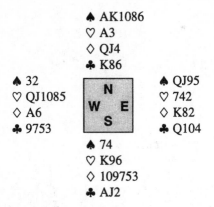

```
                    ♠ AK1086
                    ♡ A3
                    ◇ QJ4
                    ♣ K86
     ♠ 32              N          ♠ QJ95
     ♡ QJ1085                     ♡ 742
     ◇ A6          W     E        ◇ K82
     ♣ 9753           S           ♣ Q104
                    ♠ 74
                    ♡ K96
                    ◇ 109753
                    ♣ AJ2
```

To defeat the contract East must win the first round of diamonds and play a third heart. Now nothing can prevent West from regaining the lead and cashing his winners.

Should a Trump Honour be Covered?

Since the opponents have chosen their own trump suit there will be fewer occasions where it will benefit a defender to cover an honour, especially when they have supported one another (e.g. 1♡–3♡). All too often declarer will be the only one to gain, so the general advice is don't cover unless it is fairly obvious that your side might benefit.

In the following examples we are, of course, considering the trump suit.

(a)

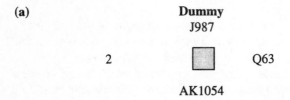

```
                    Dummy
                    J987

        2            [  ]           Q63

                    AK1054
```

No doubt declarer will play off his ace and then go to dummy and play the jack. On no account must East cover as there is nothing to be gained by doing so. With this particular holding declarer probably intends playing his king anyway but it costs nothing to test East out first.

(b)

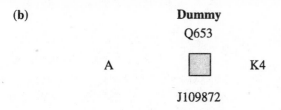

Dummy
Q653

A   K4

J109872

If the queen is played from dummy East should not cover. To do so would only gain if South held something like A109xx which, in view of declarer's chosen line of play, is improbable.

(c)

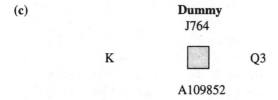

Dummy
J764

K   Q3

A109852

If the jack is led from dummy East must play low. Nothing can be gained by covering.

(d) The contract is 6♡, South having shown length in both majors. West leads the ♡2 and dummy plays the jack. Should East cover?

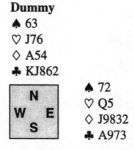

Dummy
♠ 63
♡ J76
♢ A54
♣ KJ862

♠ 72
♡ Q5
♢ J9832
♣ A973

East should not cover for two reasons. Firstly, it is inconceivable that the ♡Q will promote a trick for the defence, and secondly, declarer will surely wish to ruff some spades in dummy so that if East parts with the queen he will be unable to overruff.

This might be the full deal:

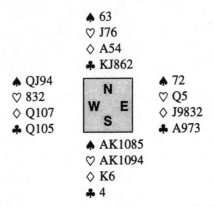

```
                    ♠ 63
                    ♡ J76
                    ◇ A54
                    ♣ KJ862
    ♠ QJ94                        ♠ 72
    ♡ 832          N              ♡ Q5
    ◇ Q107      W     E           ◇ J9832
    ♣ Q105         S              ♣ A973
                    ♠ AK1085
                    ♡ AK1094
                    ◇ K6
                    ♣ 4
```

If East does play the ♡Q on the first round, declarer will have no difficulty in ruffing two spades in dummy and making his slam. Without East's help, however, the slam is doomed.

When the trump suit has not been supported and there is only a modest offering in dummy it may be advantageous to cover. In examples (e), (f) and (g) South has just made a simple rebid of his suit.

(e)   **Dummy**
                            J5

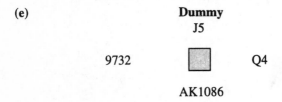

```
9732                                Q4

                    AK1086
```

The jack is played from dummy and East gains a trick for his partner by covering.

(f)

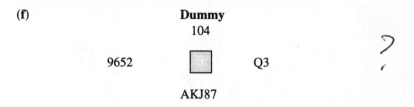

                    Dummy
                     104

     9652   Q3

                    AKJ87

The ten is played from dummy and once again East does best to cover.

(g)

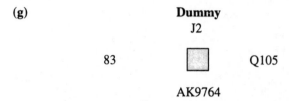

                    Dummy
                     J2

      83   Q105

                    AK9764

The jack is played from dummy and East's best prospect is to cover. He may still lose his ten later but at least he has given himself a chance.

(h)

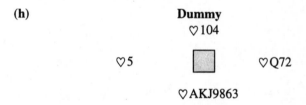

                    Dummy
                    ♡104

      ♡5   ♡Q72

                  ♡AKJ9863

South has jumped to 4♡ over his partner's bid of 1♣. When the ♡10 is played from dummy East should not cover. The bidding makes it clear that South probably has seven hearts and is just testing the water. Don't assist him.

6
SIGNALS (PETERING)

Although bridge players are not permitted to show approval or disapproval by any means other than through the medium of the cards, there are a number of ways that the cards can vividly reflect the feelings and wishes of a defender.

Perhaps the simplest way of painting a pretty picture is to play high/low to encourage. This is sometimes called Petering and is all part of *Attitude Signals* where a high card encourages and a low card discourages. What exactly constitutes a high card and what denotes a low one can only be determined by the cards that are on view and those that are played to the first trick.

Suppose you are East defending a contract of four spades and this is what you see:

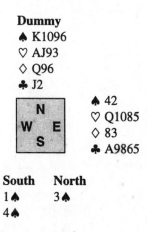

Dummy
- ♠ K1096
- ♡ AJ93
- ◇ Q96
- ♣ J2

East
- ♠ 42
- ♡ Q1085
- ◇ 83
- ♣ A9865

South	North
1♠	3♠
4♠	

Contract: 4♠ by South. Lead ◇A.

West, your partner, leads the ◊ A. It is probable that he holds the king as well so you want to give him the good news that you can trump the third round. You do this by petering – playing the eight first and then the three. Had you held 832 then of course you would have played your lowest card, the two, to discourage.

The full hand.

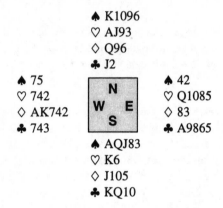

```
                  ♠ K1096
                  ♡ AJ93
                  ◊ Q96
                  ♣ J2
    ♠ 75          ┌─────────┐      ♠ 42
    ♡ 742         │    N    │      ♡ Q1085
    ◊ AK742       │  W   E  │      ◊ 83
    ♣ 743         │    S    │      ♣ A9865
                  └─────────┘
                  ♠ AQJ83
                  ♡ K6
                  ◊ J105
                  ♣ KQ10
```

On the next hand you are defending against 4♡ and once again you are East.

This is the full deal.

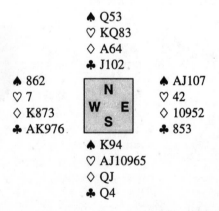

```
                  ♠ Q53
                  ♡ KQ83
                  ◊ A64
                  ♣ J102
    ♠ 862         ┌─────────┐      ♠ AJ107
    ♡ 7           │    N    │      ♡ 42
    ◊ K873        │  W   E  │      ◊ 10952
    ♣ AK976       │    S    │      ♣ 853
                  └─────────┘
                  ♠ K94
                  ♡ AJ10965
                  ◊ QJ
                  ♣ Q4
```

Contract: 4♡ by South. Lead ♣A.

On the ♣A you show your *Attitude* by playing the three: you are not enamoured. Respecting your signal, West considers the best switch and decides to attack in spades (it looks dangerous to play a diamond from the king and pointless to play his singleton heart). He chooses the ♠6 (MUD), dummy plays low, you the ten and declarer the king. When West regains the lead with the ♣K he continues with the ♠8, enabling you to make both your ace and jack which are positioned so menacingly over dummy's queen. This careful defence results in declarer going one down. Had West ignored your initial signal (♣3) and continued with a second club, dummy's ♣J would have provided a parking place for declarer's third spade. Thus with the diamond finesse right declarer would lose only two clubs and one spade.

On the next hand South plays in 4♡ and West leads the ♠K.

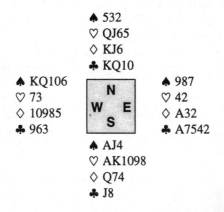

```
              ♠ 532
              ♡ QJ65
              ◊ KJ6
              ♣ KQ10
♠ KQ106                      ♠ 987
♡ 73          ┌───────┐      ♡ 42
◊ 10985       │   N   │      ◊ A32
♣ 963         │ W   E │      ♣ A7542
              │   S   │
              └───────┘
              ♠ AJ4
              ♡ AK1098
              ◊ Q74
              ♣ J8
```

On the king of spades East plays the seven and South the four. At this point West should be carefully studying the pips because unless he recognises that East has played his smallest spade, discouraging continuation, declarer may slip home. Ostensibly the seven is a big card, a come-on, and often it will be employed in that role, but with all the smaller cards accounted for West must appreciate that this is not the case here. Of course, declarer is hoping that the defenders will get their wires crossed and that West will continue with a second spade. If he does so the contract will succeed. If, however, West switches to the ◊ 10 – the most likely outcome if East's signal has been recognised – East will win the

◊A and return a spade through declarer's AJ for one down. The defence will score two spades plus both minor suit aces.

Suppose we alter the hand slightly and interchange the ♠J and ♠7 and the ♡2 for the ◊4. Now, when the ♠K is ducked, it would be essential for West to continue the suit and East should give his partner every encouragement by playing the ♠9 (East would like to signal with the ♠J but, as this is a suit contract West might have led from KQxx, East can't afford the jack).

So, *Attitude Signals* are simply a means of saying to partner, 'Yes, I like it', or 'No, I can't help you'.

When discarding you can also indicate to partner whether you like, or perhaps control, a suit by discarding a high card (the highest you can afford). This indicates that you would like the suit led if partner gets in, or perhaps where your card of entry lies. Alternatively, if partner is wondering what to discard from his own hand, then he can discard the suit in which you are strong. The other side of the coin is that when a small card is discarded it shows lack of interest, or control, in that suit.

It should be remembered that the signals you give to your partner are also available to declarer, so it is sensible to temper the desire for revealing all unless you feel that it is your partner who will be the chief, or only, beneficiary.

Another form of signal that experienced players use a great deal is the *Count Signal*. This can be especially important when declarer leads a suit and one of the defenders is wondering at what stage he should take his winner.

Let's look at the problem.

Dummy
♠ 1062
♡ 943
◇ KQJ109
♣ 72

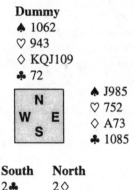

♠ J985
♡ 752
◇ A73
♣ 1085

South	North
2♣	2◇
2NT	3NT

West leads the ♡Q.

The ♡Q is allowed to win the first trick and the continuation is won by South's king. A diamond is now played to dummy's king and East ducks (if East were to take his ace immediately the whole diamond suit would be good). Declarer returns to hand via the ♠A and plays a second diamond. Should East win the ace or duck again?

Let's look at the full hand.

♠ 1062
♡ 943
◇ KQJ109
♣ 72

♠ 74
♡ QJ108
◇ 842
♣ QJ63

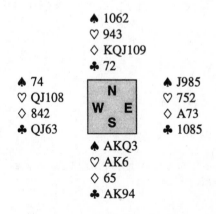

♠ J985
♡ 752
◇ A73
♣ 1085

♠ AKQ3
♡ AK6
◇ 65
♣ AK94

With all the cards on view, we can see that East must win the second diamond because declarer has no more and dummy is dead. The almost certain result will now be one down. But let us suppose that East ducks a second time, now declarer cannot be prevented from scoring three spades, two hearts, two diamonds and two clubs. So, how does East know what to do without having to rely on an educated guess? The secret lies in the cards that West plays.

With an even number of cards he should peter – play high/low. With an odd number of cards he follows in natural order. So when West followed with the two on the first round (this couldn't be the start of a peter) he was known to hold either one or three. It would be irrelevant if he held one, but in any case when the four of diamonds was played on the second round East knew that his partner started with three, and therefore declarer with two.

On the next hand an alert defence can provide declarer with a losing option.

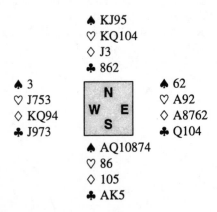

```
                 ♠ KJ95
                 ♡ KQ104
                 ♢ J3
                 ♣ 862
   ♠ 3            ┌──────┐      ♠ 62
   ♡ J753        │   N  │      ♡ A92
   ♢ KQ94        │ W   E│      ♢ A8762
   ♣ J973        │   S  │      ♣ Q104
                 └──────┘
                 ♠ AQ10874
                 ♡ 86
                 ♢ 105
                 ♣ AK5
```

Contract: 4♠ by South. Lead ♢K.

West gets away to the best lead of the ♢K. Having taken their two diamond tricks the defence switch to a club, won by South. South draws trumps in two rounds and sees that he will have to guess the location of the ♡AJ if he is to succeed.

At trick six he plays the ♡8 and West dutifully follows with the ♡7. The ♡K is played from dummy and East should duck smoothly. With several little cards missing (6, 5, 3) East can be reasonably sure that his partner has started a peter to show an even number (obviously 4; 2 would be irrelevant).

Returning to hand with a trump, declarer plays the ♡6, West the ♡3 and now everything will hinge on declarer's view of the two vital missing cards (♡A and ♡J). If he thinks West has withheld the ace he will play dummy's queen and go one down. If he thinks it is East who is holding back then dummy's ♡10 will force the ace and the ♡Q will provide the discard for declarer's losing club.

Without the use of *Count Signals* East would be uncertain as to when he should play his ♡A. For example, South might have had only one heart and one more club – then it would be essential for East to take his ♡A immediately.

There is one further signal that on occasions you will find invaluable, this is the *Suit Preference Signal* (sometimes referred to as *McKenney*). Although this signal is used in a number of different ways by experienced players, I am going to concentrate on the simple form which is related to obtaining ruffs.

You are West defending against Four Spades.

Dummy
♠ Q86
♡ KJ
◊ K10832
♣ KQ6

♠ J52
♡ Q10963
◊ 7
♣ 10753

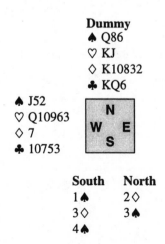

South	North
1♠	2◊
3◊	3♠
4♠	

You decide to lead your singleton diamond, hoping to get a ruff. Success! East wins with the ◇ A and returns a diamond. You ruff and collect your second trick, but what now? If you could only put partner in again you could enjoy a second ruff – and defeat the contract. Perhaps East has the ♡ A or ♣ A but which one? The secret lies in the card that East returned for you to ruff. It was the four – a very small card as the three and two are on view.

The signal works like this. Ignore the trump suit and the suit that is being led for you to ruff. That leaves just two suits. In this case hearts and clubs. If East wants a heart returned he plays a high card (calling for the higher of the two remaining suits) and if he wants a club, then he plays a low card.

Let's examine the full deal.

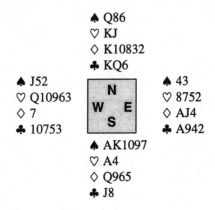

                    ♠ Q86
                    ♡ KJ
                    ◇ K10832
                    ♣ KQ6
    ♠ J52   ♠ 43
    ♡ Q10963   N   ♡ 8752
    ◇ 7   W   E   ◇ AJ4
    ♣ 10753   S   ♣ A942
                    ♠ AK1097
                    ♡ A4
                    ◇ Q965
                    ♣ J8

Had East held the ♡ A instead of the ♣ A then he would have returned the ◇ J at trick two.

One last hand shows both defenders giving *Suit Preference Signals*.

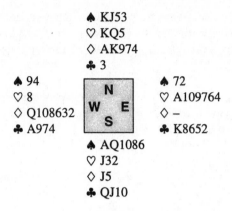

♠ KJ53
♡ KQ5
◊ AK974
♣ 3

♠ 94
♡ 8
◊ Q108632
♣ A974

♠ 72
♡ A109764
◊ –
♣ K8652

♠ AQ1086
♡ J32
◊ J5
♣ QJ10

The bidding:

West	North	East	South
–	1◊	1♡	1♠
Pass	3♠	Pass	4♠
All Pass			

West leads the ♡8 to East's ace and ruffs the heart return. What now? Well, it all depends on the size of East's heart. In fact it was a big one (♡10) suggesting that he wants to ruff a diamond. (Remember, the trump suit and the suit that is being led don't count. That leaves only diamonds and clubs to consider. A high card asks for diamonds and a low one for clubs.) So West plays the ◊10, asking for a second heart ruff. East trumps the diamond and returns the ♡9 saying that he would also like to ruff again. The ♣A and a second diamond ruff completes a remorseless defence for three down, the defence having taken the first six tricks.

Suppose East had a singleton diamond and one less club. Now, if the defence are to succeed, East must return the ♡4 and West, having ruffed, must underlead his ♣A (play the nine or seven) so as to obtain a second heart ruff. A classy defence for just one down.

Signalling in the Trump Suit

There are occasions when you would like to tell partner that you have a third trump, or alert him to the fact that you are able to ruff something. This is done by reversing the signal that you use for giving the count in a side suit.

With an *odd* number of trumps you peter i.e. play high low. With an *even* number you play in natural order. This form of signalling can be most useful in a hand like the following:

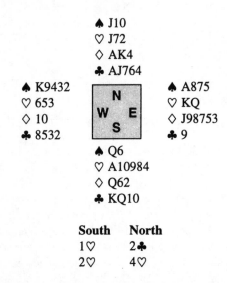

	South	North
	1♡	2♣
	2♡	4♡

West leads his singleton diamond against South's contract of four hearts. Dummy wins (♢A) and plays a heart, East following with the queen, South the ace and West ...? West should play the five. Then when declarer continues with a second heart West follows with the three. Having confirmed that he has a third trump and is able to ruff, East's task is relatively simple. He plays a diamond (the ♢J or ♢9 is best), West ruffs and then the defence cash two spade tricks for one off. Of course, South might have held six hearts, and West only two, in which case West could no longer ruff and would indicate the fact by playing his trumps in natural order. It would then be up to East to abandon the idea of diamond ruffs and simply set about taking as many tricks in spades as possible before they disappeared on dummy's long clubs.

7

THE RULE OF ELEVEN

When your partner leads the fourth highest card of a suit it is possible to determine how many cards there are in the other three hands that are better than the one led.

The formula

Deduct the pips on the card led from *Eleven*. The answer tells you how many higher cards are held by dummy, you and the declarer.

This information can sometimes be quite useful to the third player, as we shall see. Suppose this is a side-suit in a suit contract:

Dummy
◇ J85

◇ K94

West leads the ◇ 6.

Dummy plays the ◇ 8. Which card should East play?

East deducts 6 from 11 which tells him that if West's card is in fact his fourth highest there are five cards better than the six held between the other three hands. Two of these are in dummy and two with East. Therefore declarer has only one card higher than the six in his own hand and that card must surely be the ace, for West would be most unlikely to underlead his ace as an opening gambit.

This is the full layout of the suit:

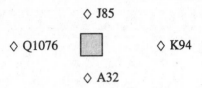

You can now see that East must play the nine in order to hold declarer to one trick in the suit. With knowledge of the *Rule of Eleven* East would no doubt find it easy to play the right card. But let us suppose he was unaware of the Rule and simply followed the usual procedure of 'third hand plays high'. Now the king would fall to the ace and subsequently dummy's jack would become a winner.

East has to be careful on the next hand but the *Rule of Eleven* comes to his assistance.

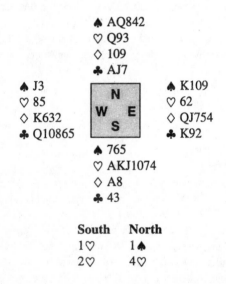

South	North
1♡	1♠
2♡	4♡

West leads the ♣6.

Looking at all four hands it is clear that declarer may lose two spades, one diamond and one club. However, on the lead of the ♣6 declarer plays the ♣7 from dummy and the ball is very much in East's court. If East makes the mistake of playing the king, declarer will subsequently be able to finesse West's queen and discard his losing diamond on dummy's ♣A.

Employing the *Rule of Eleven*, East notes that there are five cards out better than the six. Dummy has three of them and East has the other two. Armed with this knowledge, East knows that it is safe to play his nine to the first trick. The defence must now prevail.

The *Rule of Eleven* should come to East's assistance in a rather different way on the next hand.

Dummy
♠ J74
♡ 952
◊ AKJ106
♣ 109

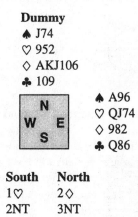

♠ A96
♡ QJ74
◊ 982
♣ Q86

South	North
1♡	2◊
2NT	3NT

West leads the ♣5.

East covers dummy's club with the ♣Q and declarer wins with the ♣K. A small diamond is played to dummy's ten and then declarer plays the ♠J.

Which card should East play? If you've made your mind up let's look at the full hand.

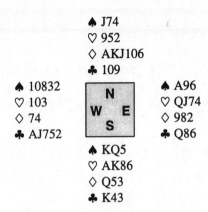

♠ J74
♡ 952
◇ AKJ106
♣ 109

♠ 10832
♡ 103
◇ 74
♣ AJ752

♠ A96
♡ QJ74
◇ 982
♣ Q86

♠ KQ5
♡ AK86
◇ Q53
♣ K43

If East does not go up with his ♠A and play a club the contract will succeed. Declarer is just testing East out, hoping he will think that a spade finesse is in the offing.

In fact, declarer can see eight top tricks and needs to pinch one quickly before the defence realise what is happening. However, East knows from the *Rule of Eleven* that South started with only one card better than the five and that card – the king – has already been played. So West's clubs are ready to be cashed and if he has a five-card suit then the contract is going down immediately. This is not the time to wait for better things.

Against a contract of four spades West leads the ♡5. What should East make of this lead?

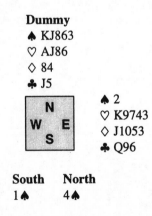

Dummy
♠ KJ863
♡ AJ86
◇ 84
♣ J5

♠ 2
♡ K9743
◇ J1053
♣ Q96

South	North
1♠	4♠

East can be certain that the lead is not the fourth highest because he can see seven cards higher than the five (5 from 11 = 6) in dummy and his own hand. When declarer plays low from dummy and follows with the two himself East can be sure that West's heart is a singleton.

This is the full hand:

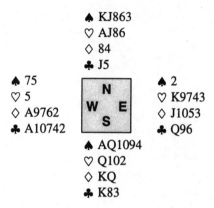

                  ♠ KJ863
                  ♡ AJ86
                  ◇ 84
                  ♣ J5

♠ 75   ♠ 2
♡ 5   N   ♡ K9743
◇ A9762   W   E   ◇ J1053
♣ A10742   S   ♣ Q96

                  ♠ AQ1094
                  ♡ Q102
                  ◇ KQ
                  ♣ K83

The king of hearts wins the first trick and East returns a heart for West to ruff. The two minor suit aces are then cashed for one down.

8
RETURNING PARTNER'S SUIT WITH THE RIGHT CARD

Communication between partners is made much more effective if the right card is played, especially when returning partner's suit. Suppose your partner leads a suit in which you have three cards, say A73. You win the ace and should return the seven – the higher of the two remaining cards. If you hold four cards or more, then you should return the original fourth highest.

Let's see some examples.

Partner leads the following suit. You win and wish to return it. The card you should play is in bold type.

K5**3**
A**2**
A8**6**4
A9**5**32
Q9**7**2

It is particularly important to return the higher of two remaining cards, as in the first example. Then when you hold a doubleton, say A3, and play back the three partner is in a strong position to read you for no more cards in the suit. You may ask, 'How is partner to know the position?' The answer is that he has to pay careful attention to the spot cards on view – those played to the first trick, those in dummy and the ones in his own hand. A review of the bidding can also clarify the probable distribution.

The hands that follow will help you to recognise what is going on.

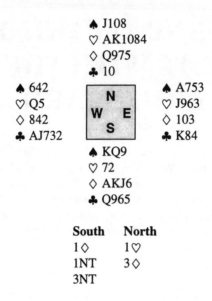

	♠ J108	
	♡ AK1084	
	◇ Q975	
	♣ 10	

♠ 642   ♠ A753
♡ Q5   ♡ J963
◇ 842   ◇ 103
♣ AJ732   ♣ K84

♠ KQ9
♡ 72
◇ AKJ6
♣ Q965

South	North
1◇	1♡
1NT	3◇
3NT	

West leads the ♣3.

The ♣K wins the first trick and East returns the ♣8, covered by the ♣9 and ♣J. What should West do next? Well, the one thing he shouldn't do is to cash the ♣A. In fact he can switch safely to any other suit, and in the fullness of time East will get in with the ♠A and play the ♣4. This third round of clubs goes through declarer's Q6 up to West's A72 and results in a two trick defeat. Had West cashed the ♣A earlier declarer would have made his contract.

So how did West know what to do? First of all, South was marked with the ♣Q because East played the king on the first round, denying the queen. Then, the ♣4 was missing. So, unless South was false-carding (i.e. playing his cards in an unnatural order), East was marked with this card. Lastly, East could not have started with four clubs as then he would have returned his original fourth highest (from K864 he would play the four at trick two).

Of course, West had to hope that his partner had a card of re-entry – not unreasonable on the bidding. As it happens North/South would have done better to finish in five diamonds, but that is not the defence's problem.

On the next hand West is able to read the position exactly but East has to be a little careful.

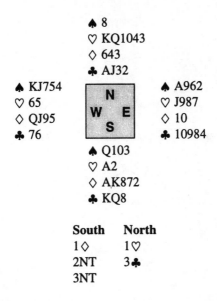

```
                    ♠ 8
                    ♡ KQ1043
                    ◇ 643
                    ♣ AJ32
    ♠ KJ754                       ♠ A962
    ♡ 65          N               ♡ J987
    ◇ QJ95      W     E           ◇ 10
    ♣ 76          S               ♣ 10984
                    ♠ Q103
                    ♡ A2
                    ◇ AK872
                    ♣ KQ8
```

South	North
1◇	1♡
2NT	3♣
3NT	

West leads the ♠5.

East wins the first trick with the ♠A and correctly returns the ♠2, West's jack capturing South's ten. West knows that East must have started with four spades because, if East's holding was A2 (the only other possible combination), then South would have begun with five spades and the bidding makes it clear that this can't be the case. West also knows that when he cashes the ♠K that South's queen is going to drop, but East must still remain alert and jettison the ♠9 under the king, otherwise the suit will be blocked. You'll notice that on this occasion it was necessary to cash out immediately as once declarer obtains the lead he has nine tricks on top.

On the next hand, also a 3NT contract, West must retain communication with his partner if there is to be any chance of defeating the game.

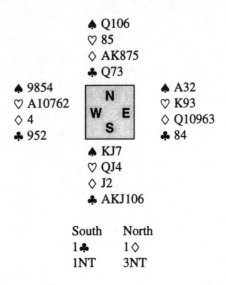

```
                    ♠ Q106
                    ♡ 85
                    ◊ AK875
                    ♣ Q73
   ♠ 9854                        ♠ A32
   ♡ A10762        N             ♡ K93
   ◊ 4          W     E          ◊ Q10963
   ♣ 952           S             ♣ 84
                    ♠ KJ7
                    ♡ QJ4
                    ◊ J2
                    ♣ AKJ106
```

South	North
1♣	1◊
1NT	3NT

West leads the ♡6.

The ♡K wins the first trick (6,5,K,4) and East returns the ♡9. Declarer covers with the ♡Q and West ...?

West should duck to preserve a link with his partner who is almost certainly marked with a third heart (where is the ♡3? And if South had started with QJ43 he might have rebid 1♡ over 1◊). This *Hold Up* play is a particularly effective gambit whenever it is necessary to maintain communication with partner. On the actual layout East regains the lead with the ♠A and plays a third heart to defeat the contract.

9
AVOID GIVING A RUFF
AND DISCARD

In normal circumstances defenders must be careful to avoid conceding a
ruff in one hand and a discard in the other when trumps remain in both
declarer's and dummy's hands. Indeed, this is a very well-known gambit
that declarers will often try to arrange in order to make their contract.

Suppose hearts are trumps and West is on lead in this end position:

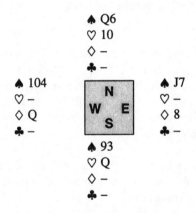

It is quite safe for West to play a spade (in which case the defence will
register one more trick), but if he makes the mistake of playing his ◇ Q,
one hand ruffs while the other discards a small spade. This way declarer
makes all the tricks.

Let's see what happens in a complete hand.

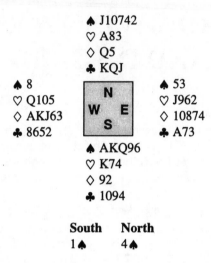

```
                    ♠ J10742
                    ♡ A83
                    ◇ Q5
                    ♣ KQJ
  ♠ 8                               ♠ 53
  ♡ Q105          N                 ♡ J962
  ◇ AKJ63      W     E              ◇ 10874
  ♣ 8652          S                 ♣ A73
                    ♠ AKQ96
                    ♡ K74
                    ◇ 92
                    ♣ 1094
```

South	North
1♠	4♠

It is clear that declarer has four losers: 2 diamonds, 1 heart and 1 club, but suppose West, having cashed the ◇AK, continues with the ◇J. Now declarer will discard a heart from one hand and ruff in the other. So a contract that started out with four inescapable losers for one down has been reduced to three losers and an easy make. The simple solution is *avoid giving a ruff and discard.*

Perhaps it might help to fully understand the *ruff and discard* factor if you place yourself in the West position on the following hand, but look at the problem from South's viewpoint.

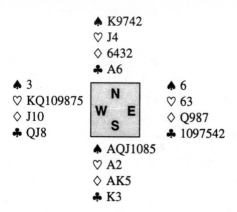

♠ K9742
♡ J4
◇ 6432
♣ A6

♠ 3
♡ KQ109875
◇ J10
♣ QJ8

♠ 6
♡ 63
◇ Q987
♣ 1097542

♠ AQJ1085
♡ A2
◇ AK5
♣ K3

Contract: 6♠ by South. West leads the ♡K.

We needn't concern ourselves with the bidding. Suffice it to say that West did his best to absorb space with a pre-emptive bid of 3♡, nevertheless North/South found their way to the spade slam.

Declarer's problem is that he seems to have two certain losers, one heart and one diamond. However, his plan should be to force West to concede him a *ruff and discard*.

The ace of hearts wins the first trick, trumps are drawn in one round and then the ♣AK and ◇AK are cashed. The moment is now right to let West have his heart trick, the ♡J losing to the ♡Q. Now look at West's problem. He can only play a heart or a club and whichever he chooses declarer will ruff in dummy and discard the ◇5 from his own hand. So declarer succeeds via this *ruff and discard* – and there is nothing West can do about it. However, the moral is: Don't concede a *ruff and discard* unless there is no viable alternative.

10
DON'T BLOCK THE SUIT

Just as declarer has to be careful not to block a suit that he wishes to run, so must a defender avoid the same trap. This is especially important in no trumps.

Dummy
♠ AQ65
♡ 1062
◇ A6
♣ 10862

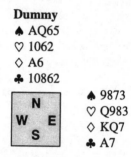

♠ 9873
♡ Q983
◇ KQ7
♣ A7

West leads the ◇ 5.

South	North
1♣	1♠
1NT	3NT

Declarer plays low from dummy and you – correctly – win with the queen. But what now? Do you sacrifice your king to the ace or do you return the ◇ 7 leaving your king as master?

Distasteful though it may be to sacrifice your king in such a ruthless manner it is nevertheless essential if you are to avoid blocking the suit. Even if you were uncertain as to the location of the jack, the king would invariably be the right card to play. However, in this case the Rule of Eleven tells you that South has only one card better than the five and it really can't be the jack as that would leave West with the 10985(2). With this holding he would surely lead the ten, not the five.

The full deal:

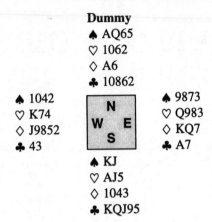

Dummy
♠ AQ65
♡ 1062
◇ A6
♣ 10862

♠ 1042
♡ K74
◇ J9852
♣ 43

♠ 9873
♡ Q983
◇ KQ7
♣ A7

♠ KJ
♡ AJ5
◇ 1043
♣ KQJ95

With the diamond suit unblocked, you regain entry with the ♣A and lead your ◇7 for West to run his winners.

On the next hand it is West who has to be careful not to block the suit that he has led.

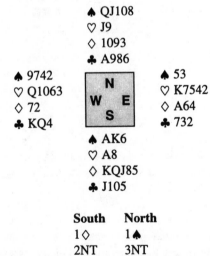

♠ QJ108
♡ J9
◇ 1093
♣ A986

♠ 9742
♡ Q1063
◇ 72
♣ KQ4

♠ 53
♡ K7542
◇ A64
♣ 732

♠ AK6
♡ A8
◇ KQJ85
♣ J105

South	North
1◇	1♠
2NT	3NT

Against 3NT West leads the ♡3. Declarer tries the ♡J from dummy but East covers with the king and South ducks. East now plays the ♡4 (his original fourth highest) to South's ace and it is the moment of truth for West. If he follows with the ♡6 the suit will be blocked and the defence will collect just three hearts and the ◇A. If, however, he unblocks his ♡10 the contract will fail. East will win the ◇A, play the ♡2 to West's ♡Q and overtake the ♡6 with the ♡7 for one down.

By paying careful attention to the pips, West will notice that the ♡2 has not appeared and this, together with declarer's duck for just one round, is consistent with East holding five hearts and South two.

Although the necessity to unblock is more likely to arise in no trumps it can also be essential in a suit contract. Here is an example:

```
                    ♠ 8653
                    ♡ 74
                    ◇ KQ
                    ♣ KJ986
  ♠ KQJ109                        ♠ A72
  ♡ A852          N               ♡ 63
  ◇ 96         W     E            ◇ 87532
  ♣ 72            S               ♣ Q103
                    ♠ 4
                    ♡ KQJ109
                    ◇ AJ104
                    ♣ A54
```

West	North	East	South
–	–	–	1♡
1♠	2♣	2♠	3◇
Pass	3♡	Pass	4♡
All Pass			

West leads the ♠K and if he follows with the ♠Q and East fails to unblock the ace the contract will succeed. Declarer ruffs and plays the ♡K. West ducks, wins the continuation and carries on with the force in spades. However, on the ♠A declarer refuses to ruff and instead discards a small club.

Unable to continue with another spade, East's next card is no problem. Declarer wins, draws trumps and claims the remainder of the tricks. Note the difference when the ♠A is played at trick two (West might have foreseen the problem and helped his partner by playing a lower spade on the second round thus forcing East to contribute the ace). In with the ♡A, West continues plugging away with spades and, when declarer has to trump a second time, West has one more trump than South and the contract fails.

11
REFUSING THE OVERRUFF

Extra tricks can often be made by refusing to overruff. Consider the following. A side suit is led of which both declarer and West are void and in each case West gains a trick by declining to overruff.

Hearts are trumps and East leads a master diamond.

(a)

West's hearts	Declarer's hearts
AJ	KQ1098

Declarer ruffs with the king. West discards and will then make *two* trump tricks instead of only one.

(b)

West's hearts	Declarer's hearts
K103	AQJ98

Declarer ruffs with the queen. West refuses to overruff and will then make *two* trump tricks.

(c)

West's hearts	Declarer's hearts
A932	KQJ1075

Declarer ruffs with an honour. West declines to overruff and subsequently makes *two* trump tricks instead of just the ace.

Here is an example from play.

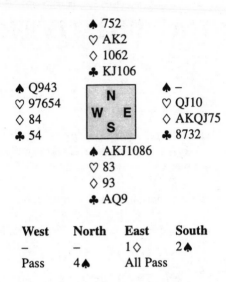

♠ 752
♡ AK2
◇ 1062
♣ KJ106

♠ Q943   ♠ –
♡ 97654   ♡ QJ10
◇ 84   ◇ AKQJ75
♣ 54   ♣ 8732

♠ AKJ1086
♡ 83
◇ 93
♣ AQ9

West	North	East	South
–	–	1◇	2♠
Pass	4♠	All Pass	

Against South's four spades West leads a diamond and East plays three top cards in the suit. Declarer ruffs the third round with the ♠10 and the spotlight falls on West. If he overruffs with the ♠Q the defence will take no more tricks and the contract succeeds. If, however, West declines to overruff he will subsequently come to two trump tricks and defeat the game.

12
TRUMP PROMOTION

A common defensive ploy is for one defender to play a suit in which both declarer and defender's partner are void, thereby promoting a trump to winning rank. The following combinations appear in this scenario.

	Trumps
K alone	over AQ etc
Qx	over AK etc
Jxx	over AKQ etc
10xxx	over AKQJ etc

The hands that follow will help to clarify this technique.

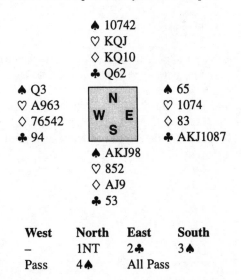

♠ 10742
♡ KQJ
◇ KQ10
♣ Q62

♠ Q3
♡ A963
◇ 76542
♣ 94

♠ 65
♡ 1074
◇ 83
♣ AKJ1087

♠ AKJ98
♡ 852
◇ AJ9
♣ 53

West	North	East	South
–	1NT	2♣	3♠
Pass	4♠	All Pass	

Against South's contract of four spades, East takes two club tricks and knows that declarer can ruff the third round. However, there is no better continuation and in fact a third round of clubs promotes West's ♠Q to winning rank. If South ruffs with a low trump West overruffs and if he plays the ace or king West's queen must subsequently take a trick.

On the next hand East has to be a little more careful.

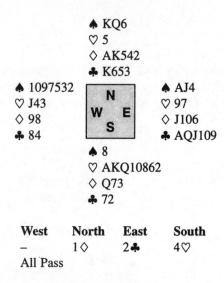

	♠ KQ6	
	♡ 5	
	◊ AK542	
	♣ K653	

♠ 1097532   ♠ AJ4
♡ J43   ♡ 97
◊ 98   ◊ J106
♣ 84   ♣ AQJ109

           ♠ 8
           ♡ AKQ10862
           ◊ Q73
           ♣ 72

West	North	East	South
–	1◊	2♣	4♡
All Pass			

Against four hearts West leads the ♣8 and East knows that this must be a doubleton or singleton (with three small West would lead the middle card MUD), so he wins with the nine and cashes the ace. It seems a simple matter to continue with a third round of clubs and promote a trump trick for West but this defence is not good enough as declarer will simply discard his losing spade. To defeat the contract East must first cash his ♠A and then play a third club.

There is one more situation of which a defender must be aware. Suppose the cards fall like this:

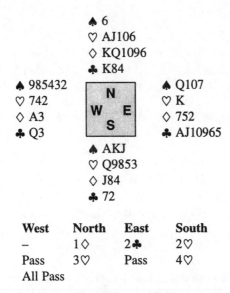

```
              ♠ 6
              ♡ AJ106
              ◇ KQ1096
              ♣ K84
♠ 985432              ♠ Q107
♡ 742      N          ♡ K
◇ A3    W     E       ◇ 752
♣ Q3       S          ♣ AJ10965
              ♠ AKJ
              ♡ Q9853
              ◇ J84
              ♣ 72
```

West	North	East	South
–	1◇	2♣	2♡
Pass	3♡	Pass	4♡
All Pass			

Against four hearts West leads the ♣Q, covered by the king and ace. East cashes the ♣J, but what should he play next? It looks routine to play a third club but if declarer ruffs high – which seems likely – then West is unable to overruff and the cat will be well and truly out of the bag. Even the most unenterprising declarer will now, surely, reject the trump finesse and pin his hopes on East's 'marked' king being bare.

So East should switch to a spade at trick three and not reveal the position. A suspicious declarer may wonder why East did not continue with a third club but, whatever conclusion he comes to, at least East will not have provided an exact blueprint of the layout.

Another exciting form of trump promotion is the *uppercut*. Like a boxer who may score a knock-out blow with this one punch, a bridge player can sometimes defeat his opponents when any other stratagem would not even cause a ripple. As the name might suggest, the *uppercut* occurs when a defender ruffs with a highish trump forcing declarer to use an even higher one, which in turn promotes a trick for defender's partner.

Let's see the *uppercut* in action.

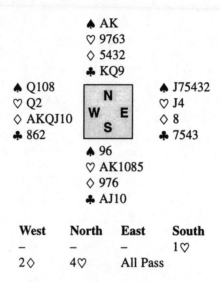

♠ AK
♡ 9763
◊ 5432
♣ KQ9

♠ Q108
♡ Q2
◊ AKQJ10
♣ 862

♠ J75432
♡ J4
◊ 8
♣ 7543

♠ 96
♡ AK1085
◊ 976
♣ AJ10

West	North	East	South
–	–	–	1♡
2◊	4♡	All Pass	

Against South's contract of four hearts West starts with four rounds of diamonds. On the fourth round East ruffs with the ♡J (the *uppercut*) in the hope that he might promote a trick for his partner. When declarer has to overruff, West's ♡Q becomes a defensive trick and the contract is defeated.

Sometimes it takes *two uppercuts* to achieve a knock-out. East/West combined well on the following hand and were handsomely rewarded when an apparently laydown contract was defeated.

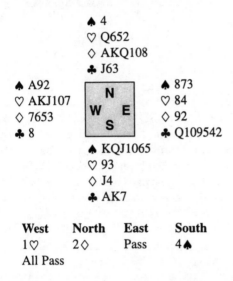

```
                    ♠ 4
                    ♡ Q652
                    ◇ AKQ108
                    ♣ J63
    ♠ A92                          ♠ 873
    ♡ AKJ107          N            ♡ 84
    ◇ 7653         W     E         ◇ 92
    ♣ 8               S            ♣ Q109542
                    ♠ KQJ1065
                    ♡ 93
                    ◇ J4
                    ♣ AK7
```

West	North	East	South
1♡	2◇	Pass	4♠
All Pass			

Against four spades West started with two top hearts and then continued with a third round. Although declarer played low from dummy, East ruffed with the ♠7 and declarer overruffed with the ♠10. West won the ♠K with ♠A and played a fourth heart, East administering the coup de grâce by ruffing with his last spade, the eight. Declarer overruffed with the ♠J but now West's ♠9 was promoted to winning rank (♠92 over ♠Q65).

13
DISCARDING

When you are unable to follow suit in a no trump contract, or in a suit contract when you do not wish to trump, you have to make a discard and this is unquestionably one of the most difficult areas of defensive play. It would be nice to say, 'Throw away what you don't want and keep what may be useful' but this would be an over simplification, although there is more than a grain of sound advice in following such a philosophy. Perhaps the biggest difficulty is determining what can be spared and what is actually going to be of use. Here are a few guidelines.

1. Try to retain the same number of cards as the cards in a suit held by dummy, or the cards held by declarer if you can assess that from the bidding.

(a)

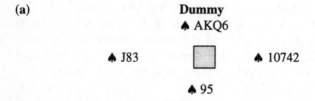

Dummy
♠ AKQ6

♠ J83   ♠ 10742

♠ 95

Only East is guarding dummy's spades. If he discards *one*, all dummy's spades become winners.

(b)

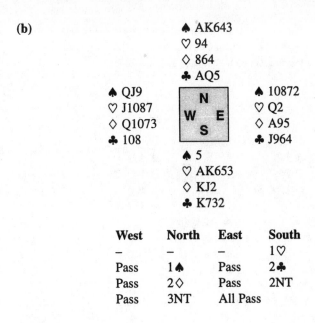

♠ AK643
♡ 94
◊ 864
♣ AQ5

♠ QJ9   ♠ 10872
♡ J1087   ♡ Q2
◊ Q1073   ◊ A95
♣ 108   ♣ J964

♠ 5
♡ AK653
◊ KJ2
♣ K732

West	North	East	South
–	–	–	1♡
Pass	1♠	Pass	2♣
Pass	2◊	Pass	2NT
Pass	3NT	All Pass	

West leads the ◊ 3.

South plays in 3NT. East wins the diamond lead and returns the suit, West winning with the queen. West plays a third diamond to clear the suit and at trick four South plays a low heart. West wins this trick with ♡10 and cashes the thirteenth diamond. What should East discard? The clue, as in most cases of this type, is in the bidding. South is likely to have a four-card club suit and for this reason East should retain the same number. Maybe West can guard the spades. He certainly won't be able to guard the clubs if South has four. If East makes the mistake of discarding a club the contract will succeed. If instead he throws a spade, or even his ♡Q, declarer is likely to finish one down.

Sometimes you are faced with an unenviable choice of discards, but the principle of keeping the same number of cards as in the long suits that you see in dummy may come to your rescue.

(c)

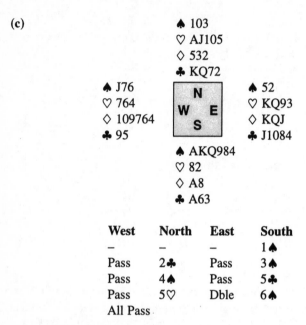

♠ 103
♡ AJ105
◇ 532
♣ KQ72

♠ J76
♡ 764
◇ 109764
♣ 95

♠ 52
♡ KQ93
◇ KQJ
♣ J1084

♠ AKQ984
♡ 82
◇ A8
♣ A63

West	North	East	South
–	–	–	1♠
Pass	2♣	Pass	3♠
Pass	4♠	Pass	5♣
Pass	5♡	Dble	6♠
All Pass			

Contract: 6♠ by South.

In response to his partner's double, West leads the ♡6 which runs to the ten and queen. East switches to the ◇K which is won by the ace. Three top spades follow, dummy discarding a diamond and East doing likewise (◇J) as he can't spare anything else. But when a fourth spade is played East has an unenviable choice to make. Dummy has parted with another diamond, but what should East do? Following the principle of keeping dummy's length covered, East should discard his ◇Q and hope that his partner has the ten. This defence defeats the contract, but let us suppose that East had discarded a club or a heart. In the first case dummy's long club would provide the twelfth trick, and in the second declarer would play a heart to the ace and ruff a heart, leaving dummy's ♡J as master.

2. It is often necessary to retain a link to partner's hand, especially when he has established winners that he is waiting to cash.

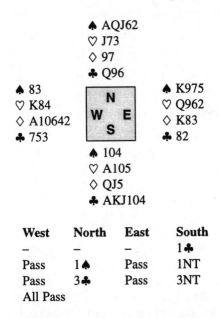

	♠ AQJ62	
	♡ J73	
	◊ 97	
	♣ Q96	

♠ 83		♠ K975
♡ K84	N	♡ Q962
◊ A10642	W E	◊ K83
♣ 753	S	♣ 82

	♠ 104	
	♡ A105	
	◊ QJ5	
	♣ AKJ104	

West	North	East	South
–	–	–	1♣
Pass	1♠	Pass	1NT
Pass	3♣	Pass	3NT
All Pass			

West leads the ◊4 against South's contract of 3NT. East wins the ◊K and returns the ◊8, West correctly withholding his ace to preserve communications. With eight tricks on top declarer will have to rely on the spade finesse, but first he cashes his five club tricks. West should discard one heart and one spade but now the spotlight falls on East who has to find three discards. In fact he is not really under too much pressure as he can spare two spades and one heart. But he must retain that small diamond so that when he wins with the ♠K he can then put partner in to cash his diamond tricks.

3. Whenever possible avoid blanking a worthless suit, or even discarding from it if there are other cards available that can just as easily be spared.

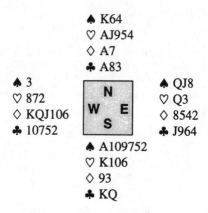

<pre>
                    ♠ K64
                    ♡ AJ954
                    ◇ A7
                    ♣ A83
  ♠ 3   ♠ QJ8
  ♡ 872   N   ♡ Q3
  ◇ KQJ106   W   E   ◇ 8542
  ♣ 10752   S   ♣ J964
                    ♠ A109752
                    ♡ K106
                    ◇ 93
                    ♣ KQ
</pre>

Contract: 6♠ by South.

North/South propel their way to six spades and West leads the ◇K. Declarer wins in dummy, plays a spade to the ace, cashes the ♣KQ and then plays a spade to dummy's king. He now discards his losing diamond on the ♣A and gives East his spade trick. Up to this point West has had to find two discards and although superficially it may appear that his small hearts are expendable he should not discard any of them!

Although those worthless hearts are of no use to West, he doesn't want to expose the position to declarer – that he has nothing of value in the suit and therefore any missing honour (♡Q in this case) is with his partner. Furthermore, for the moment West has plenty of easy discards that he can make in diamonds and clubs. Only if the position arises whereby he is the sole defender guarding a diamond in dummy should he then part with a heart.

Suppose East returns a diamond at trick eight. South ruffs and starts cashing his remaining spades. Now West must hang on to those three small hearts and hopefully declarer will missguess the position of the queen.

4. If declarer draws trumps before ruffing a suit in dummy you may conclude that he has no losers to ruff.

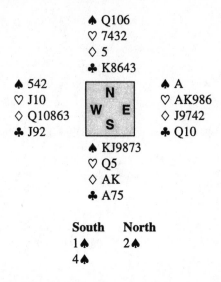

♠ Q106
♥ 7432
♦ 5
♣ K8643

♠ 542
♥ J10
♦ Q10863
♣ J92

♠ A
♥ AK986
♦ J9742
♣ Q10

♠ KJ9873
♥ Q5
♦ AK
♣ A75

South	North
1♠	2♠
4♠	

West leads the ♡J against South's contract of four spades. East wins the ♡AK and plays a third round which declarer ruffs high. The ♠A takes the next trick and South ruffs the fourth heart. Three top spades follow and West has to make a critical discard. He has already parted with two small diamonds on the hearts and now has to discard a club or another diamond on declarer's last spade. It must be correct to discard a third diamond as declarer could have ruffed a losing diamond in dummy had he wished. The fact that he didn't do so strongly suggests that there was no loser to ruff. By clinging on tenaciously to his fragile club holding West is able to defeat the contract.

5. In desperate circumstances it is sometimes necessary to unguard a vital honour card in order to give the defence their best chance.

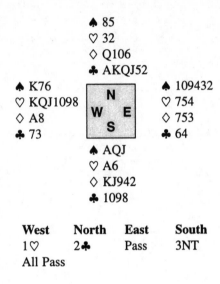

	♠ 85	
	♡ 32	
	◊ Q106	
	♣ AKQJ52	

♠ K76		♠ 109432
♡ KQJ1098	N	♡ 754
◊ A8	W E	◊ 753
♣ 73	S	♣ 64

	♠ AQJ	
	♡ A6	
	◊ KJ942	
	♣ 1098	

West	**North**	**East**	**South**
1♡	2♣	Pass	3NT
All Pass			

West leads the ♡ K.

After West's opening bid of one heart, South becomes the declarer in 3NT, rather than in the more comfortable contract of 5♣ or 5◊. The ♡K is allowed to hold and the ♡Q is taken, perforce, by the ace. Declarer now starts on the club suit and West can see that he will have to find four discards. If he goes for the soft option of parting with 1 diamond, 1 spade and 2 hearts declarer will almost certainly make his contract by throwing West in with the ◊A. Having cashed his two heart winners, West will then have to lead away from his ♠K giving declarer his ninth trick (2 spades, 1 heart and 6 clubs). So West should plan to blank his ♠K. His discards might go: ♠6, ◊8, ♠7 and ♡9 – a small false card to further the illusion that he started with only five hearts and therefore has just the J10 left. If declarer now plays as envisaged he will go down, thanks to intelligent discarding by West.

14
PLAYING THE CARD YOU ARE KNOWN TO HOLD

When declarer takes a finesse against you, it sometimes happens that you can give a misleading impression of your full holding in that suit.

(a)

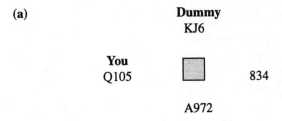

Dummy
KJ6

You
Q105

834

A972

Declarer leads low towards dummy and plays the jack, successfully finessing your queen. When he next cashes the king you should contribute the queen – the card you are known to hold. Perhaps on the way back to his hand, reading you for the Q5 alone, he will lead the six to his nine ...

You should always give declarer the chance to go wrong provided you have a lower card that has become promoted to the same rank as the card finessed.

(b)

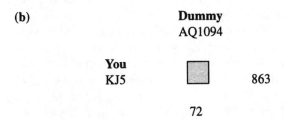

Dummy
AQ1094

You
KJ5

863

72

Declarer leads towards dummy and when West follows with the five he plays the queen. Next he cashes the ace and it is at this point that you should follow with the king – the card you are known to hold. The jack is now the same rank as the king but declarer can't be sure who holds this card.

Let us transfer this suit to a full hand so that we can consider declarer's problem when West makes life difficult by playing the card he is known to hold.

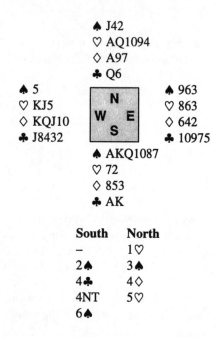

           ♠ J42
           ♡ AQ1094
           ◇ A97
           ♣ Q6

♠ 5   ♠ 963
♡ KJ5   ♡ 863
◇ KQJ10   ◇ 642
♣ J8432   ♣ 10975

           ♠ AKQ1087
           ♡ 72
           ◇ 853
           ♣ AK

South	North
–	1♡
2♠	3♠
4♣	4◇
4NT	5♡
6♠	

West leads the ◇K against South's contract of six spades. The ◇A wins and is followed by the ♠AK. When the spades fail to break declarer leaves the ♠J in dummy and plays a heart to dummy's queen, successfully finessing West's king. The ♡A follows and it is important that West contributes the ♡K – the card he is known to hold. The ♡10 is played next and when East follows with the eight this is the moment of truth. Declarer has to guess whether to run the ♡10, on the assumption that East holds the jack, or trump and hope that West follows suit. If West plays the ♡J on the ace declarer knows that the king will fall when he plays a third round.

15
PLAY THROUGH STRENGTH ROUND TO WEAKNESS

If there are no other priorities in the offing, it is invariably correct to play through strength – especially short suit strength – and round to weakness.

Suppose there are these two side suits in dummy (North).

$$\heartsuit \ 743$$
$$\diamondsuit \ AQ10$$

If West is on lead without any obvious play to make, a lead through dummy's diamond strength would be indicated. But if East is on lead in a similar position to his partner, a heart would probably be best – through declarer's presumed strength round to dummy's weakness. The next two deals illustrate the point.

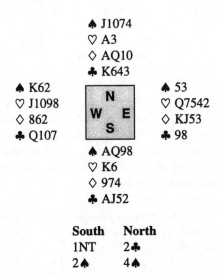

```
              ♠ J1074
              ♡ A3
              ◇ AQ10
              ♣ K643
  ♠ K62                    ♠ 53
  ♡ J1098      N           ♡ Q7542
  ◇ 862      W   E         ◇ KJ53
  ♣ Q107       S           ♣ 98
              ♠ AQ98
              ♡ K6
              ◇ 974
              ♣ AJ52
```

South	North
1NT	2♣
2♠	4♠

West leads the ♡J against South's contract of four spades. Declarer wins
in hand and returns the suit to dummy's ace. The ♠J loses to West's ♠K
and West should now switch to a diamond – through dummy's strength. If
he fails to do this, perhaps playing a second spade instead, East becomes
in real danger of being end-played. The play may go: two more rounds of
spades, ♣K and club finesse, losing to West's queen. West now switches
to a diamond and East takes the ◊10 with ◊J, but now East has no safe
card of exit and will have to give declarer his tenth trick. Had West
switched to a diamond at trick four, East could have won and got off lead
safely with a second trump.

On the next hand it is East who has to make the critical move.

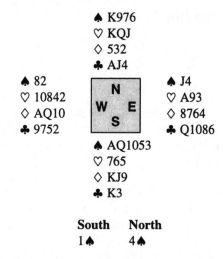

```
              ♠ K976
              ♡ KQJ
              ◊ 532
              ♣ AJ4
  ♠ 82           N        ♠ J4
  ♡ 10842                 ♡ A93
  ◊ AQ10    W       E     ◊ 8764
  ♣ 9752        S         ♣ Q1086
              ♠ AQ1053
              ♡ 765
              ◊ KJ9
              ♣ K3
```

South	North
1♠	4♠

West leads the ♡2 against South's contract of four spades. East wins with
the ace and now success or failure depends on how East continues. He
should switch to the ◊7 or ◊8 (East plays a high card as he doesn't want
his partner to think that he has an honour in this suit). West wins and can
exit safely with a second heart. Subsequently he will come to two more
diamond tricks to defeat the contract.

If East makes the mistake of returning a heart at trick two, or any suit other
than diamonds round to weakness, declarer wins, draws trumps,
eliminates clubs and hearts and then plays a diamond towards his hand.
West wins this trick but is now end-played and the contract succeeds.

16
AVOIDING A BATH COUP

The Bath Coup, a legacy from the days of Whist, is a tactic used by declarer to try and tempt you into his trap. West leads the king in the following situations:

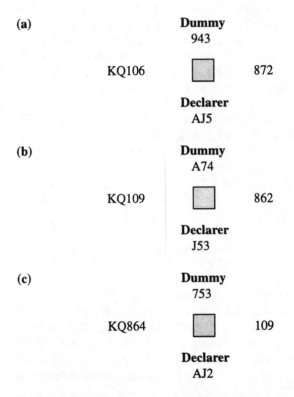

(a)

Dummy
943

KQ106   872

Declarer
AJ5

(b)

Dummy
A74

KQ109   862

Declarer
J53

(c)

Dummy
753

KQ864   109

Declarer
AJ2

In all three cases declarer refuses to take the king with his ace and West is faced with a dilemma. Should he continue the suit or not? If he does so declarer will gain an extra trick.

Having seen the problem, how should West avoid the trap? Most of the time the answer is to be found in the card contributed by partner.

Against no trump contracts, East should play the jack (if he has it) on partner's king because the opening lead will usually be from a suit headed by the KQ10. When East fails to play the jack, West can assume that declarer has it and therefore he must find a switch.

Against a suit contract, the problem is less straightforward because there is no necessity for the opening leader to have the ten with his KQ. From KQ862 the lead would be the king against a suit contract but the six, the fourth highest, against no trumps. However, partner's card on the first trick will frequently be revealing. In (a) and (b) East will play the two – a discouraging card if ever there was one. In (c) he will play the ten which will look like the beginnings of a peter showing a doubleton, but this card should still deny the jack. With J10 (against a suit or no trumps) East would play the jack. So, with the jack marked in the South hand West should be able read the position for what it is.

A bigger problem faces West if the cards fall like this. Let's say the contract is four hearts and this is the spade suit:

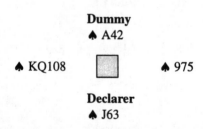

Dummy
♠ A42

♠ KQ108   ♠ 975

Declarer
♠ J63

West leads the ♠K, declarer ducks in dummy – hoping for a continuation – and East does his best to discourage by playing the five. However, declarer attempts to muddy the waters by following with the six. West may note that the three is missing and will then have to decide whether it is his partner who is encouraging, or South indulging in a spot of chicanery. Where everyone plays an honest card West should have no difficulty in deciding to switch.

On the following hand it is imperative that East informs his partner that he is not being set up for a Bath Coup.

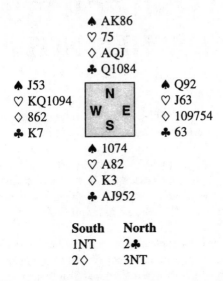

	♠ AK86	
	♡ 75	
	◇ AQJ	
	♣ Q1084	
♠ J53		♠ Q92
♡ KQ1094		♡ J63
◇ 862		◇ 109754
♣ K7		♣ 63
	♠ 1074	
	♡ A82	
	◇ K3	
	♣ AJ952	

South	**North**
1NT	2♣
2◇	3NT

West finds the best lead of the ♡ K against 3N, and, no matter which cards are played to this trick, declarer intends to duck. So everything depends on East. If he fails to contribute the ♡J West will no doubt assume that declarer's holding is AJ2. Of course, a switch would be fatal for the defence as they would no longer be able to defeat the contract. When East follows with the ♡J, West continues the suit with confidence and the game is doomed – the defence taking four hearts and one club.

So the simple rule is this. When partner leads the king against a no trump contract it is correct to contribute the jack if you hold it. The only exceptions are when the opening lead appears to be from a short suit, or where dummy's holding is such that, by wasting your knave, dummy's intermediate cards may become established.

17
PLAYING FOR RUFFS AND WHEN NOT TO

With a singleton in the hand it is always tempting to play for ruffs but there are some important guidelines that should be borne in mind.

1. The trump holding should be suitable, i.e it should have spare trumps available to do the business. Axx, Kxx or xxx are ideal holdings. A concentration of honours such as AQ, KQ or KJ etc obviously suggest that a different attack would be more profitable.

2. There must be reasonable prospects of partner being able to obtain the lead. If the bidding indicates that partner is unlikely to have a quick enough entry to give you a ruff, more harm than good comes from the singleton lead, it being only too likely to place the missing cards and distribution for declarer.

3. It is generally a mistake to play for ruffs with a strong trump holding. With trump suits like AJ9x, K10xx, Q109x or even J98x it is usually best to play a forcing game, i.e. play on your long suit with the intention of weakening declarer's trumps.

The following hands illustrate these points.

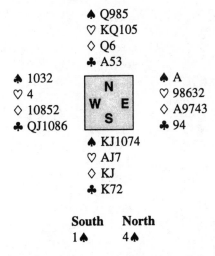

♠ Q985
♥ KQ105
♦ Q6
♣ A53

♠ 1032
♥ 4
♦ 10852
♣ QJ1086

♠ A
♥ 98632
♦ A9743
♣ 94

♠ KJ1074
♥ AJ7
♦ KJ
♣ K72

South	North
1♠	4♠

Unless West leads his singleton heart, hoping that East will be able give him a ruff, four spades will be an easy make. In fact, declarer will only lose one spade and one diamond, the club loser going away on the long heart.

When the ♥4 is led, East will get in with the ♠A and return the ♥9 (a suit preference signal asking for the return of a diamond, see Chapter 6). West ruffs and dutifully returns a diamond to East's ace. When East now plays a third heart West scores his second ruff and the contract is defeated.

On the next hand the opening lead may make quite a difference.

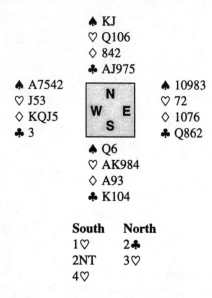

```
                    ♠ KJ
                    ♡ Q106
                    ◊ 842
                    ♣ AJ975
♠ A7542         ┌─────────┐      ♠ 10983
♡ J53           │    N    │      ♡ 72
◊ KQJ5          │  W   E  │      ◊ 1076
♣ 3             │    S    │      ♣ Q862
                └─────────┘
                    ♠ Q6
                    ♡ AK984
                    ◊ A93
                    ♣ K104
```

South	North
1♡	2♣
2NT	3♡
4♡	

West should reason that his partner is unlikely to be able to get in to give him a ruff if he leads his singleton. This being the case more harm than good would come out of opening up the suit. Instead, he leads ◊ K. Now success for declarer will depend on his guess in clubs. Maybe he'll get it right, but if he doesn't he will lose two diamonds, one spade and one club. At least West will not have helped him on his way.

On this last hand, if West follows sound basic principles, the contract will be defeated. Let's see what happens.

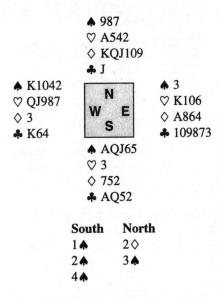

♠ 987
♡ A542
◇ KQJ109
♣ J

♠ K1042
♡ QJ987
◇ 3
♣ K64

♠ 3
♡ K106
◇ A864
♣ 109873

♠ AQJ65
♡ 3
◇ 752
♣ AQ52

South	North
1♠	2◇
2♠	3♠
4♠	

Suppose an untutored West leads his singleton diamond against South's contract of four spades. East will win and give him his ruff immediately, but then the only other trick the defence will make is the ♠K. So the contract succeeds.

Now let us assume that West is aware of the fact that it doesn't pay to play for ruffs with such a strong trump holding, so he leads the ♡Q. The ♡A wins and the spade finesse loses to West. A second heart forces declarer to ruff. When declarer later loses the lead to the ◇A he is forced again, transferring trump control to West. The contract now stands little chance.

18
REQUESTING AN UNDERLEAD

Since it is incorrect to peter – play high low – with the doubleton queen (although it is correct with Jx, 10x etc), the play of the queen on partner's lead of the ace has a special meaning. It requests partner to underlead the suit – i.e not to cash his king but to play a low card on the next round – and, of course, guarantees the knave – unless the queen is singleton.

This play is especially useful when it is imperative for the partner of the leader to obtain the lead, or when you wish to avoid the honours clashing together. The next two examples illustrate these points.

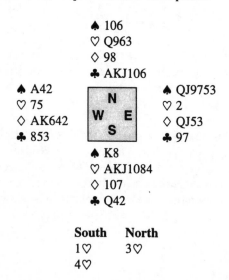

```
                    ♠ 106
                    ♡ Q963
                    ◇ 98
                    ♣ AKJ106
   ♠ A42                             ♠ QJ9753
   ♡ 75          N                   ♡ 2
   ◇ AK642    W     E                ◇ QJ53
   ♣ 853          S                  ♣ 97
                    ♠ K8
                    ♡ AKJ1084
                    ◇ 107
                    ♣ Q42
```

South	North
1♡	3♡
4♡	

West leads the ◇A against South's contract of four hearts and if he then continues with the ◇K there is no way the contract can be defeated. Indeed, if he doesn't cash the ♠A declarer will make an overtrick. However, if East plays the ◇Q on his partner's ◇A – requesting an underlead – West will be happy to oblige with a small diamond to East's jack. Then the ♠Q will ensure two spade tricks for the defence and the contract goes one down.

On the next hand it is essential for West to underlead his king at trick two for a different reason.

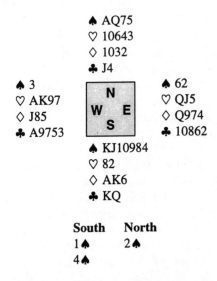

                    ♠ AQ75
                    ♡ 10643
                    ◇ 1032
                    ♣ J4

    ♠ 3   ┌─────────┐   ♠ 62
    ♡ AK97   │   N   │   ♡ QJ5
    ◇ J85   │ W   E │   ◇ Q974
    ♣ A9753   │   S   │   ♣ 10862
                   └─────────┘
                    ♠ KJ10984
                    ♡ 82
                    ◇ AK6
                    ♣ KQ

        South   North
        1♠   2♠
        4♠

West leads the ♡A against South's contract of four spades. So far so good, but if he now happens to continue with the ♡K declarer will make his contract by ruffing a third round and establishing dummy's ♡10 for a diamond discard.

Note what happens when East plays the ♡Q on West's ♡A – a request to underlead his ♡K. A small heart is won by the ♡J and now the ♡10 will no longer become a winner. In due course declarer will lose two hearts, one club and one diamond for one down.

19
HELPING PARTNER TO AVOID MISTAKES

By the very nature of the game partner is sure to make mistakes, but a thoughtful accomplice can often help him to minimise them, just as you hope he will help you to minimise yours. There are a number of ways in which this can be achieved, and indeed whole books have been devoted to the subject, but for our purposes some general advice and three example hands will have to suffice.

One thing that will help partner is if you learn to play the correct card. For example, if you hold the KQ1064 it is, of course, correct to lead the king; if partner plays the suit to you, you would endeavour to win with the queen – unless the jack is in dummy and dummy plays low when you would try to win with the ten. This may sound relatively simple and straightforward but you would be surprised how many players pull any card from their hand, safe in the knowledge that it makes no difference to them, and quite oblivious of the fact that partner is receiving misleading information which may later result in his making an unnecessary mistake.

It is worth remembering that correct cards are played entirely for partner's benefit so that he can read the position and act accordingly. They may sometimes help declarer but that is not the object of the exercise. It's just an unfortunate by-product. In fact, if we didn't have to bother about information for partner we could produce a plethora of false cards hoping to confuse declarer. Indeed, this is sometimes an acceptable ploy but if we did it routinely I guess that we would run very short of partners!

Another tip is to pay careful attention to partner's lead: both the suit and the size of the card should be carefully memorised.

Initially it will not always have a special significance, but as the hand develops it should be possible to place it in a definite category. A lead from honours, from shortage or perhaps from rubbish. If it is not immediately clear the mist may have eased by the time partner plays again to the same suit – providing you can recall what his card was in the first place.

Finally, there are moments when *one* of the defenders is in a privileged position to judge exactly what is required to sink the contract. When this happens he must be prepared to Mastermind the whole operation.

On the following hand, if West is left to his own devices, it would be difficult for him to read the position correctly. Maybe on a good day he would rise to the occasion but East should not let him waste his mental energies on this when he knows all the answers himself.

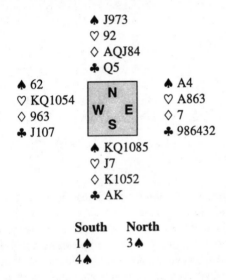

♠ J973
♥ 92
♦ AQJ84
♣ Q5

♠ 62   ♠ A4
♥ KQ1054   ♥ A863
♦ 963   ♦ 7
♣ J107   ♣ 986432

♠ KQ1085
♥ J7
♦ K1052
♣ AK

South	North
1♠	3♠
4♠	

West leads the ♥K.

Only East knows that he has a singleton diamond and a sure entry with the ♠A. So he should overtake the ♥K with ♥A and play his diamond. No doubt declarer will play a low spade from dummy, but East goes in immediately with the ♠A and puts his partner on play with the ♥Q to give him his diamond ruff. Two hearts, one spade and a diamond ruff adds up to four tricks – just enough to defeat the contract.

On the next hand, East sees one small chance to wrong-foot the declarer. For once it means giving partner some misleading information – but it's all in a good cause and definitely comes under the heading of 'Helping Partner'.

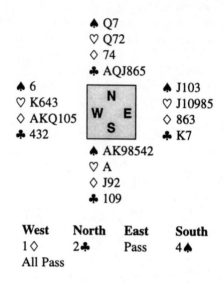

```
                        ♠ Q7
                        ♡ Q72
                        ◊ 74
                        ♣ AQJ865
        ♠ 6                          ♠ J103
        ♡ K643         N             ♡ J10985
        ◊ AKQ105    W     E          ◊ 863
        ♣ 432          S             ♣ K7
                        ♠ AK98542
                        ♡ A
                        ◊ J92
                        ♣ 109
```

West	North	East	South
1◊	2♣	Pass	4♠
All Pass			

West leads the ◊ A.

If the defence follow Momma/Poppa lines, declarer will lose just two diamonds and one club. However, East not only assists his partner to find the right attack, he hatches a diabolical plot as well. On the ◊ A he follows with the eight and on the ◊ K he completes a peter with the three. Thinking that East must hold a doubleton diamond, West continues with a third round. Declarer has also noted the peter and duly ruffs with dummy's ♠ Q. Now, when the spades fail to break and the club finesse is wrong, the contract is one down.

On the final hand East made a mistake that allowed the contract to roll home, but was it really his fault, or was West more culpable for failing to foresee East's problem? Let's have a look.

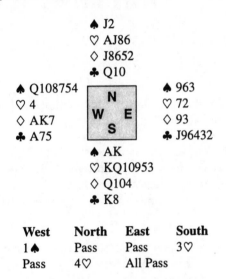

♠ J2
♡ AJ86
◇ J8652
♣ Q10

♠ Q108754
♡ 4
◇ AK7
♣ A75

N
W E
S

♠ 963
♡ 72
◇ 93
♣ J96432

♠ AK
♡ KQ10953
◇ Q104
♣ K8

West	North	East	South
1♠	Pass	Pass	3♡
Pass	4♡	All Pass	

West led the ◇A against South's contract of four hearts. When East petered with the 93 West was delighted to give him a ruff. On lead at trick four East played a spade, the suit his partner had bid, but then the roof fell in. Following the ♠A, declarer drew trumps and discarded his two clubs on dummy's master diamonds. So the contract was made, West going to bed with his ♣A.

Although East played the wrong suit when in with the diamond ruff, he did what virtually all other players would have done in his position. His error could have been avoided so easily had West thought of removing the problem before it reached his partner. All he had to do was to cash the ♣A before giving East his ruff.

20
COUNTING

There is little doubt that counting is the most difficult task for a novice but the rewards are so huge that trying to master it really is worth quite a bit of effort. Whether playing the hand or defending, an accurate knowledge of the distribution and the whereabouts of the high cards can solve many a problem that would otherwise be a pure guess. So what I would like to do is to try and make the counting exercise more acceptable. Make it easier to understand and perhaps transform it into a habit that comes almost naturally.

Let's start with the point count. In order to arrive at the best contract the opposition have to exchange information, and in doing so their point count is frequently announced in unequivocal terms. All we have to do is to tune in and store the information away and wait to see if it can be used to our advantage.

Quite often the information we have gained will be useless to us. The declarer simply cashes his tricks and only when the contract is safely in the bag does he condescend to allow us the leftovers. Nevertheless, a defender should always carry out the small exercise of estimating how many points are held by his partner.

You are East in the following examples.

1.
       ♠ K865
       ♡ 9753
       ◇ 964
       ♣ J5

South	North
1NT	3NT

Well, they haven't given away too much but if South has 13 points (the no trump shows 12-14), North 13 and East 4, that leaves West with 10.

Dummy

♠ Q107
♡ AK4
◇ 52
♣ AQ1096

West leads the ◇ Q and when dummy goes down, East sees that he has to make a slight adjustment. As dummy holds 15 points (15+13+4 = 32) West is likely to hold about 8 points, not 10.

On this particular hand, as we shall see, the small exercise in calculating partner's points does nothing to help our defence.

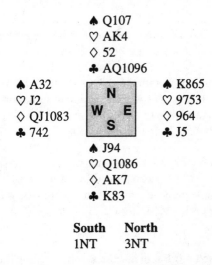

♠ Q107
♡ AK4
◇ 52
♣ AQ1096

♠ A32
♡ J2
◇ QJ1083
♣ 742

♠ K865
♡ 9753
◇ 964
♣ J5

♠ J94
♡ Q1086
◇ AK7
♣ K83

South	North
1NT	3NT

Obviously declarer takes the first eleven tricks and the defence the last two. Just for the exercise note how West should also estimate his partner's points. Opener 13, dummy 15 and West 8. That totals 36, leaving East with 4.

With a slight alteration to this hand we get:

2.

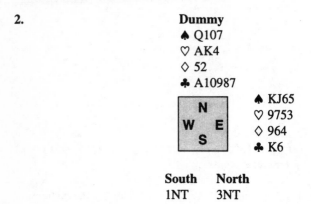

Dummy
♠ Q107
♡ AK4
◇ 52
♣ A10987

♠ KJ65
♡ 9753
◇ 964
♣ K6

South	North
1NT	3NT

West leads the ◇ Q.

The same bidding and the same lead, but this time East reasons that West has about 7 points, 3 of which are obviously the ◇ QJ.

Declarer wins the first trick with the ◇ A (the ◇ K would have been better) and plays the ♣ Q to East's ♣ K. East now has an important decision to make. Should he return his partner's suit (often a wise move) or should he switch to a spade hoping his partner has Axx?

South is marked with the ◇ AK and probably the ♣ J as well as the ♣ Q. If he has no picture card in hearts he will hold the ♠ A, but if he has the ♡ J or ♡ Q, or both, there is no way that he can hold the ♠ A as that would give him too many points (◇ AK, ♣ QJ, ♡ J and ♠ A = 15, or with the ♡ Q instead of ♡ J = 16).

There is another factor. If South has the ♠ A he has nine tricks: four clubs, two diamonds, two hearts and one spade. So it is reasonable for East to assume his partner's seven points are the ♠ A and ◇ QJ. He switches, therefore, to ♠ 4. Partner wins with the ace and returns the suit for one down.

The full hand is:

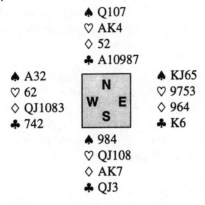

```
                    ♠ Q107
                    ♡ AK4
                    ◇ 52
                    ♣ A10987
  ♠ A32            ┌─────────┐        ♠ KJ65
  ♡ 62            │    N    │        ♡ 9753
  ◇ QJ1083        │ W     E │        ◇ 964
  ♣ 742           │    S    │        ♣ K6
                   └─────────┘
                    ♠ 984
                    ♡ QJ108
                    ◇ AK7
                    ♣ QJ3
```

Now you can see that unless East does his sums he won't appreciate how easily the contract can be defeated. Yet, if he is aware of *partner's* points it is not too difficult to draw the right conclusions.

'Well,' you might say, 'that's in no trumps when the point count is usually precise, but what about suit contracts?'

Try this for size.

3.
Dummy
♠ 1093
♡ Q104
◇ 75
♣ AKJ86

```
┌─────────┐      ♠ Q862
│    N    │      ♡ 752
│ W     E │      ◇ A863
│    S    │      ♣ 73
└─────────┘
```

South	North
1♡	2♣
2♡	3♡
4♡	

West leads the ◇2.

South's rebid of two hearts shows a minimum hand, but then when his partner invites game (3♡) he accepts (4♡), so he can't be completely minimum. Place him with around 14 points. Dummy has 10 and East 6 so that leaves West with around 10.

West is certain to have an honour in diamonds because he led the ◇2. He might even have the KJ but he won't have the KQ because then he would have led the ◇K. The ♣Q would be an unfortunate card in the West hand but it is quite likely, and if South has top hearts (probable) West will have at least one high honour in spades to make up his quota of points. If East assesses the position like this he will win the first trick with the ◇A and switch to the ♠2.

The full hand.

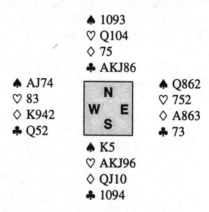

```
              ♠ 1093
              ♡ Q104
              ◇ 75
              ♣ AKJ86
♠ AJ74                        ♠ Q862
♡ 83          N               ♡ 752
◇ K942     W     E            ◇ A863
♣ Q52         S              ♣ 73
              ♠ K5
              ♡ AKJ96
              ◇ QJ10
              ♣ 1094
```

South will try the ♠K but the defence now take two spades and two diamonds for one down. Had East returned a diamond at trick two the contract would not have been defeated.

Now let us turn out attention to the distribution, although high card points and tricks available to declarer will always be a pertinent factor for the defence.

In the following sequences the defenders should make a preliminary estimate of the suit lengths, but be prepared to make minor adjustments as the hand develops. When a major suit is bid first and followed by a minor suit it usually shows five-four. When a major suit is the subject of a jump rebid (1♡–1♠–3♡) the opener will usually have a six-card suit.

(a)

South	North
1♡	1♠
2♣	

South probably has five hearts and four clubs.

(b)

South	North
1♠	2◊
2♡	3NT
4♡	

South has at least ten cards in the majors.

(c)

South	North
1♡	2◊
3♣	

South has five hearts and probably four clubs.

(d)

South	North
1♡	2◊
3♡	

South is likely to have a six-card heart suit and, of course, a better than minimum hand.

With the preliminary estimate of the distribution often available after opener's rebid, the remaining gaps usually fall into shape as the play proceeds.

Let's look at some hands.

Dummy
♠ K5
♡ 962
◇ Q83
♣ KQ1095

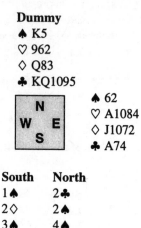

♠ 62
♡ A1084
◇ J1072
♣ A74

South	North
1♠	2♣
2◇	2♠
3♠	4♠

West leads the ♡3.

If East takes the view that South has five spades and four diamonds the lead of the ♡3 (as the ♡2 is in dummy West presumably has a four-card suit) marks South with two hearts and, therefore, also two clubs. This becomes important when declarer plays a club towards the dummy.

The defence take the first two heart tricks and declarer ruffs the third round. Before drawing trumps declarer plays a club to dummy's king, West contributing the two and East ...? Knowing that declarer has a doubleton club, East should duck smoothly. Maybe declarer will return to hand and play a second club but if he misguesses this time (plays ♣Q) he will go down.

The full hand.

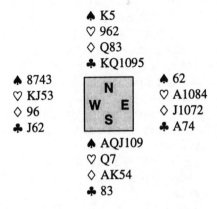

                ♠ K5
                ♡ 962
                ◇ Q83
                ♣ KQ1095

♠ 8743   ♠ 62
♡ KJ53   N   ♡ A1084
◇ 96   W   E   ◇ J1072
♣ J62   S   ♣ A74

                ♠ AQJ109
                ♡ Q7
                ◇ AK54
                ♣ 83

If East is not aware of the distribution and plays his ♣A on the first round, declarer will win the return, draw trumps and test the diamonds. When they fail to break he has an easy club finesse for his contract.

It is West who has to make a critical decision on the next hand after opening with a bid of two diamonds, which he hasn't quite got.

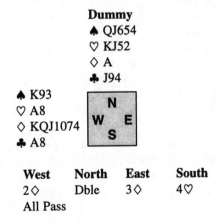

            Dummy
            ♠ QJ654
            ♡ KJ52
            ◇ A
            ♣ J94

♠ K93
♡ A8   N
◇ KQJ1074   W   E
♣ A8   S

West	North	East	South
2◇	Dble	3◇	4♡
All Pass			

On the ◇K East follows with the ◇3. A heart to declarer's nine is taken by the ace and West returns a heart, everyone following. Declarer now plays the ace and another spade to West's king, East contributing the two and then the eight. What should West do now? Should he exit with a third spade, play a diamond or cash the ♣A in the hope that he can pick up two club tricks before declarer's losing clubs are discarded on dummy's spades?

Only an inside knowledge of the distribution will help West to make the right decision. The bidding and play to the diamond suit indicates that East has five diamonds, therefore a ruff and discard at this stage could be fatal. Cashing the ♣A would be all right as long as East holds the ♣K but would otherwise be disastrous. Playing a third spade would permit declarer to make three discards (it looks as though East has three spades – no peter – and declarer two). So if declarer has five hearts, one diamond and only two spades, he must have five clubs, and three discards will still leave him with two clubs. Thus it is not necessary for West to get trigger-happy and cash his ♣A.

This is the full deal.

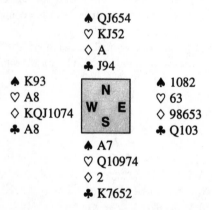

```
              ♠ QJ654
              ♡ KJ52
              ◊ A
              ♣ J94
   ♠ K93          N          ♠ 1082
   ♡ A8                      ♡ 63
   ◊ KQJ1074   W   E         ◊ 98653
   ♣ A8            S         ♣ Q103
              ♠ A7
              ♡ Q10974
              ◊ 2
              ♣ K7652
```

If West manages to work out the distribution he will play a third spade and the declarer, forced to play clubs himself, will lose two more tricks for one down. This is a rather complicated hand but it does illustrate how important it is for the defenders to keep careful track of the distribution.

Perhaps it is worth mentioning that with a slight adjustment of the East and South hands it would be absolutely vital for West to switch to the ace and another club. For example, the hands might be like this:

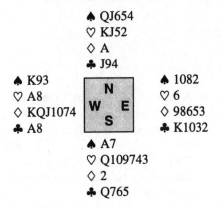

```
              ♠ QJ654
              ♡ KJ52
              ◇ A
              ♣ J94
♠ K93                        ♠ 1082
♡ A8          N              ♡ 6
◇ KQJ1074   W   E            ◇ 98653
♣ A8          S              ♣ K1032
              ♠ A7
              ♡ Q109743
              ◇ 2
              ♣ Q765
```

Now if East/West don't take their two club tricks they will find themselves making only one. The difference here is that South has one more heart and one less club – information that is readily available to West.

With practice, it soon becomes a profitable habit to estimate where the missing points are located. Equally worthwhile, although rather more taxing, is to pinpoint the distribution. An inferential count can often be made from the auction and then as the hand develops the missing bits can be slotted into place. Sometimes the complete count can be accurately inferred after the opening lead; e.g. South, the eventual declarer, bids two suits, marking him with at least nine cards in those suits. West leads a telling card which maybe indicates that he holds four cards in a third suit. Dummy's cards and East's cards added together will then give the number of cards in that third suit held by declarer. Let's say it is three. In that case, with nine cards already known, or at least presumed, declarer has only a singleton in the fourth suit.

Counting is the complete antidote to gazing at the ceiling for divine inspiration, or wistfully dreaming of how nice it would be to have a hot line to Mystic Meg!

GLOSSARY

BALANCED HAND
A hand in which the suits are evenly, or nearly evenly, distributed. 4-3-3-3, 4-4-3-2 or 5-3-3-2 are the hand patterns in this category.

CASHING
Cashing tricks means taking those that are there and available to be collected without having to resort to any special play.

CONTRACT
The final bid, which is followed by three passes, becomes the Contract. Making the Contract is winning the number of tricks promised by the bid.

DECLARER
Declarer is the player whose responsibility it is to fulfil the contract. He has become declarer because he bid the suit in which he is playing first.

DISCARDING
You discard when you are unable to follow suit and throw a card from another suit.

DISTRIBUTION
How the cards are divided in a hand according to lengths and shortages – sometimes called *shape*.

DOUBLETON
Two cards only in a suit.

DOWN
When a player goes down he has failed to fulfil his contract and consequently has to concede a penalty.

DRAWING TRUMPS
Taking the opponents' trumps away from them.

DUCKING — Deliberately refusing to take a trick by playing a low card when a higher one is available. The idea is that the high card(s) may be used to greater advantage later in the play.

DUMMY — Dummy is declarer's partner who takes no part in the play of the hand. The dummy hand is the hand that is exposed on the table.

ELIMINATING — Playing out winners, and perhaps trumping losers as well, from dummy's and declarer's hands so that the opposition when thrown on lead are unable to play the suit or suits concerned to advantage.

END-PLAY — Throwing a player on lead usually towards the end of the game – so that, hopefully, he is forced to concede an extra trick.

ENTRIES — High cards or trumps that enable a player to reach his partner's hand.

ESTABLISHING — Making a suit good, either by ruffing the losers or conceding a trick or tricks to achieve the same purpose.

FINESSING — Playing towards split honours with the hope of capturing the missing honour(s), e.g. lead small to AQ, AQ10, KJ, AJ10. But a finesse can also be taken at much lower levels, e.g. lead small to 108 hoping to find the 9 well placed.

HOLD-UP — Deliberately not taking a trick with a high card when one is available.

INTERIOR SEQUENCE — A sequence headed by an honour with a higher honour at the head of the suit but missing the next honour, e.g. AQJ10, KJ109, Q1098. The QJ10, J109 and 1098 in these settings are known as interior sequences.

MAJOR SUITS	Spades and Hearts.
MINOR SUITS	Diamonds and Clubs.
OPENER	The first player to bid.
OPENING LEAD	The original lead made by the defender on declarer's left.
OVERCALL	A bid made over an opponent's bid.
PASS	The same as *no bid.*
PETER	A signal to partner by playing high/low, say the 8 followed by the 5.
POST-MORTEM	A term applied to the discussion of the hand at the conclusion of play.
RUFFING	Trumping when having none of the suit led.
SEQUENCE	A run of three cards or more with no break in the consecutive order, e.g. AKQ, KQJ, QJ10, 9876.
SIDE SUIT	A suit other than the trump suit held by declarer or dummy.
SINGLETON	One card only in a suit.
SLAMS	Twelve winning tricks constitutes a Small Slam and all thirteen tricks a Grand Slam.
TENACE	Two cards in the same suit, one of which is higher than the missing card and one lower e.g. AQ, KJ, 108, 97.
TREBLETON	Three cards only in a suit.
VOID	Having no cards in one of the suits.